LAUNDRY LOVE

LAUNDRY LOVE

Finding Joy in a Common Chore

Patric Richardson

with Karin B. Miller

FLATIRON
BOOKS
NEW YORK

www.flatironbooks.com

Illustrations courtesy of Zach Harris, birdsandkings.com

Designed by Donna Sinisgalli Noetzel

Library of Congress Cataloging-in-Publication Data

Names: Richardson, Patric, author.
Title: Laundry love : finding joy in a common chore /
Patric Richardson with Karin B. Miller.
Description: First edition. | New York : Flatiron Books, 2021. |
Identifiers: LCCN 2020031678 | ISBN 9781250235190 (hardcover) |
ISBN 9781250235206 (ebook)
Subjects: LCSH: Laundry.
Classification: LCC TT985 .R52 2021 | DDC 648/.1—dc23
LC record available at https://lccn.loc.gov/2020031678

Our books may be purchased in bulk for promotional,
educational, or business use. Please contact your local bookseller
or the Macmillan Corporate and Premium Sales Department
at 1-800-221-7945, extension 5442, or by email at
MacmillanSpecialMarkets@macmillan.com.

First Edition: 2021

10 9 8 7 6 5 4 3 2 1

To Granny Dude, who had enough love for the entire world, and I was lucky enough to be in the center of it. —P

AUTHORS' NOTE

Patric Richardson and Karin B. Miller are not responsible for any damages arising from laundering while under the influence (though a little vodka *can* go a long way with laundry), using bluing on a white wedding dress, allowing a wool sweater to float openly during a warm-water wash cycle (or alternatively to dry in a dryer), laundering acts of God, etc. The reader assumes sole responsibility for laundry processes. Doing laundry isn't rocket science, but it is domestic science. The Laundry Evangelist action figure sold separately.

CONTENTS

INTRODUCTION

I have a vivid memory from when I was two years old: My great-uncle Quinn is holding me up in the air so that I can gaze down upon my mom's washing machine, and I am mesmerized by the clothes swimming in circles in the sudsy water.

This is so fascinating to me, in fact, that watching clothes being washed becomes one of my favorite toddler activities. Whenever I visit someone's house, I ask to inspect the laundry room—I want to see *every* washing machine. I realize that my neighbors, relatives, and friends have lots of different models: the wringer washer, the Gyratator, the rare locomotive.

While some parents might have found my fascination a bit embarrassing, my mom thought it was hilarious. And so, for my third birthday, she and my dad gave me a kid-size washing machine—and because it was the 1970s, the color was harvest gold. It had a window on top, just like my mom's (because, let's face it, my dad didn't do laundry), and it had a handle on the side that I could crank to make my clothes mimic the action of a real washing machine. I was over the moon.

My love of laundry only deepened as I grew older. I learned how to wash and dry my own clothes before I was ten. In my teens, I taught myself to iron like a picky pro, creating razor-sharp creases in my khakis. And at university, with a love of dry-clean-only clothes while on a college-student budget, I sought out my textile professors to find out if I could wash my wool sweaters and pants myself. (I suspected I could—after all, people had been wearing wool clothing all over the world since long before the invention of dry cleaning.) Yet I never would have imagined that my initial curiosity would lead me to study, explore, and experiment with various methods of caring for clothes, let alone become a laundry expert and the pioneer of a "Laundry Camp" that would help thousands of interested participants.

Now, with decades of experience using conservation washing and drying techniques on everything from vintage designer gowns to my favorite lived-in Levi's, I'm sharing my professional advice with you in these pages, covering all of my best tips, tricks, and techniques for mastering the art of laundry. My mission is to help you make laundry faster, cheaper, kinder to the environment, and more fun.

I'll also share stories about many people I love—especially the women who raised me, as they sparked my interest in textiles, taught me how to care for clothes, and showed me love and affection from the time I was small.

So sit back, take a (laundry) load off, and get ready: I'm

about to transform your sorting, washing, and drying routines. And, for my big finish, I'll teach you everything you need to know about removing stains—chocolate! red wine! dog pee!

Remember that pile of dirty clothes on the floor? It's calling to you! There's no time like the present—so let's get started.

MY CAST OF CHARACTERS

With any great Russian novel, you'll likely find a cheat sheet of characters, reminding you who everyone is, particularly the secondary folks who only pop up every now and then. For *Laundry Love*, I thought I should do the same, especially since so many of my stories star women. ("Wait a second—who's Ruby again?") So, taking my cue from Tolstoy, my list includes personal descriptions; each one's relationship to myself; and sartorial, or clothing, preferences (of course). Feel free to refer back to the list whenever needed.

Granny Dude: While my mom's mom's given name was Irene, I always called her Granny Dude. She was the matriarch of our family and well respected by everyone she knew. This book wouldn't have happened without her. My love for her is absolute. Think of her as the queen mother.

Mom: Her friends know her as Wilma, but she's always Mom to me. Mom loves beautiful clothes and beautiful living, she gave me an incredible childhood, and she influenced me in many ways with her sense of style. If you want to know what a true Southern lady looks like, just look her up. She's like Jackie Kennedy with a Southern drawl.

Nancy: Nancy is married to my dad, but calling her my step-mother sounds cold and impersonal. From the time I met her when I was twelve, she's been warm and loving. If you visit, she'll have your favorite food waiting. Think of her as Florence Henderson in the role of Mrs. Brady.

Granny Martha: Old-fashioned and Appalachian, my dad's mom doted on me and truly would have let me get away with murder. In my mind's eye, I always think of her in a day dress and an apron, cooking soup beans and corn bread—the stuff of legend. She would have fit in perfectly on *The Waltons*.

Roberta: I lucked out with Roberta, Nancy's mom, as well—she was warm like Nancy and I loved her. An upholsterer by trade, she was infinitely talented with fabric and thread, so we shared that passion. The spunky character of Idgie in *Fried Green Tomatoes* reminds me of Roberta. In a more modern time, she would've beaten the heck out of the glass ceiling.

Ibb: Granny Dude's best friend's name was actually Ibbie—how wonderful is that? Fun and spirited with a mischievous side, she always wore great perfume and made the best red velvet cake—for my birthday, Thanksgiving, and Christmas. Combine the personality of Auntie Mame and the style of Aunt Bee of *The Andy Griffith Show* and you've got Ibb.

Ruby: Ruby lived on the other side of the hill from where I grew up, and was sophisticated and worldly. She taught me lessons about style and polish that I still use today. When I first read Truman Capote's *A Christmas Memory*, I immediately thought of my relationship with Ruby, but you can think of her as Katharine Hepburn.

Louise: My mom's middle name is Louise because of this

Louise—a friend of Granny Dude and Granddad. Louise treated my mother like a really lucky niece, and I grew up thinking of her as a bonus grandmother. Imagine her like Julie Andrews as Maria von Trapp—but maybe Bea Arthur, too, since Louise could command a room.

The Professors: Three University of Kentucky professors had a profound influence on me. Mrs. Karen Ketch taught fashion and merchandising, had a big laugh, and loved to talk about clothes, fashion, and the runway. Dr. Kim Spillman offered an intellectual approach to apparel and the garment industry, and I learned a great deal from her about why we wear what we wear, which has had a major impact on my approach to dressing. And Dr. Elizabeth Easter knew absolutely everything about textiles, from warp to weft; she opened my eyes to the many uses of fabrics and their care and sparked my obsession with luxury fibers. (I still to this day want a vicuña coat!)

Marion: Ross's mom (see below for more on Ross) was the daughter of two Sámi parents, who emigrated from Finland to the United States and ended up living in northern Minnesota. While I only knew her for a few years before she passed away, I loved her sense of fun and her mischievous wit.

Finally, there's one more person I must mention—my love, Ross. Ross is the funny one, the one who allows me to follow my passions, the one who makes me want to do laundry, or bake, or breathe. When I met him in 2005, he told me that I should write a book and, fast-forward, here it is. The book, like my story, isn't complete without Ross in it. Think of—well, I think of perfection, so you can think of whomever that is to you.

GLOSSARY

acetate: This semisynthetic fabric mimics silk, is used occasionally for party dresses and suit linings, and is made from cellulose (derived from wood pulp). Its downside? Both acetone and high heat can make it melt.

argyle: Originating from Scotland, this pattern of overlapping diamonds shows up on lots of fabrics, but is seen most often on sweaters and colorful socks.

duds: I looked up the origin of this term, which is slang for *clothes*, and found it's Middle English. I grew up with this word—am I that old?

dungarees: A charming and old-fashioned term, *dungarees* is simply another word for jeans.

ikat: This beautiful Indonesian fabric is made by twisting yarns very tightly, tie-dyeing them, and then weaving them into intricate graphic patterns with a variegated finish.

knit: Created by knitting, this textile is flexible and durable, thanks to its looping yarn.

paisley: A Persian pattern of curved teardrop shapes, paisley is commonly used in ties and scarves.

plaid: This pattern of horizontal and vertical bands intersects at right angles. Tartan plaids, like those used to make kilts, are common examples.

vicuña: This fabric is made from the wool of the vicuña, a Peruvian pack animal similar to a llama. The animals are shorn and their wool is made into luxurious yarns that are both incredibly warm and light. Vicuña fabrics are some of the most expensive textiles in the world.

warp: This term refers to the vertical threads in a woven fabric.

weft: This term refers to the horizontal threads in a woven fabric.

woven: This fabric, made by weaving, has both horizontal and vertical threads, and is usually created on a loom. Wovens are usually stronger and less stretchy than knits.

LAUNDRY LOVE

1

Don't Let Your Clothes Tell You What to Do

Look after your laundry, and your soul will look after itself.

—W. SOMERSET MAUGHAM,
PLAYWRIGHT AND NOVELIST

Dry clean only. Wash in cold water. Handwash. Dry flat. Spot-wash only. Blah, blah, blah.

When it comes to cleaning, our clothes are bossy. Their tags bully us into time-sucking techniques, and before we know it, each article of clothing is trying to tell us what to do—and none of it is simple.

It's time to say goodbye to all that. Soon you'll know exactly how to care for all your textiles—meaning anything made of cloth, from clothes and bedding to bath towels and table linens—and you'll be able to do it all at home. Anything, and I mean anything, can be washed at home. And I'm going to teach you how.

When I say "anything," that includes all your clothes: cashmere sweaters, wool suits, social dresses, and whatever else you can think of. *Grandma's fur coat?* Yep. *A wedding dress?* You bet. Plus pillows, curtains, rugs, and more.

Now, imagine the fluffiest, whitest towels you've ever wrapped yourself in. Imagine crawling into bed between peppermint-scented sheets. Imagine finally getting to wear your favorite *fill-in-the-blank* again after I teach you how to remove its stains. Most important, imagine being able to do all this for yourself and for the ones you love—simply and easily.

That's the promise of this book: It will transform laundry—that chore you previously tolerated, or perhaps hated—into something you enjoy, look forward to, maybe even love. And for those of you who, like me, already love laundry, I promise you'll love it even more.

Did I mention this book is basically free? That's because you'll never pay those whopping dry-cleaning bills again if you follow my advice. Plus, you'll save loads of time—and time is money, so you'll have even more money in your pocket. Unless, of course, you really *want* to pack up your clothes, wait in line to drop them off, remember to pick them up, wait in line again to pick them up, haul them back home (hoping a few don't slide to the floor on the way)—all the while paying a pretty penny for the privilege of doing so. Think of all that cash you'll save—every month, every year—by eliminating this errand. *Cha-ching!*

Now, let's say you have a significant other and a couple of kids.

You're likely running seven loads of clothes every week at roughly an hour and twenty-five minutes per washed-and-dried load. That adds up to a grand total of ten hours. *Ten hours a week!*

I'll slash that time to *four hours and ten minutes* just once a week—less than half of what the average family currently spends doing their laundry. What are you going to do with all that extra time? Write a novel? Open a new business? Nap? Think of the options!

Included in that calculation of saved time is the spot-cleaning I teach in this book, which adds just five minutes, at most, per load. Your stains will disappear, your clothes will be cleaner, and you'll wear them more often. Most people don't spot-treat stains—they just hope for the best. And hope, as they say, is not a strategy.

OK, so you're saving piles of money and lots of time. What else is there to offer?

Well, my washing tips will wow you. For example, how about those old jeans you love so much that are too faded to wear beyond your front door? You can rescue them: Mix a tablespoon of good, old-fashioned bluing in a basin of warm water, and then let your jeans soak overnight. The denim will drink up the bluing, and *presto!* You've just salvaged your jeans. (Not quite blue enough yet? Just repeat the process, little by little, for the best results, until your jeans are just the way you like them.)

There are many more great tips to come. Most important, the advice I share in these pages will simplify your laundry life, and maybe even your actual life. Because the last thing we need to do is to complicate our busy, overcommitted lives even further. Easy peasy is my mantra.

My Love Language

Let me give you a bit of background.

The first real garment I ever owned was a camel hair overcoat purchased by my mom. It boasted a fur collar and a matching fur hat. Because what else do you buy a three-year-old boy growing up in the heart of Appalachia? My mom still has this extraordinary garment, tucked away in a closet. She bought it at Nasser's, a fine clothing store in Huntington, West Virginia. I didn't know it then, but this was likely the beginning of my love affair with textiles.

It was also the start of a childhood, and a life, filled with extraordinary women who taught, inspired, and supported my interests and me from the very beginning. I was incredibly lucky. I lived on a hill dotted with the homes of the first of these women—my mom, of course; my beloved Granny Dude, who lived next door; Ibb, my grandma's best friend, who indulged me like a favorite grandchild; and our globe-trotting, glamorous neighbor, Ruby. All of them, every last one, doted on me and spoiled me. In truth, through no deserving of my own, I was treated like a little deity.

If I'd loved the violin, they would have signed me up for lessons and clapped at recitals until their hands hurt. If I'd loved football, they would have driven me to practices, cheered me on at games, even chewed out refs who'd dared to make questionable calls.

But I loved clothing, and so they cultivated my passion by taking me shopping, indulging me with fine clothes (for example, a classic pair of brown leather cowboy boots at age three), and teaching me how to care for them.

But what I learned from them were not just the how-tos.

In his books, author Gary Chapman teaches five "love

languages"—ways to express and experience love. Mine is service. That's what caring for clothes meant for my grandmother, for my mom, and now for me. Far beyond obligation, service is the way I show others love—whether I'm ironing my husband's shirts, washing our vintage table linens in preparation for a party, or decorating our home for Christmas.

Changing our mindsets from simply cleaning clothes to caring for others is key to changing our attitudes about laundry from drudgery to love. In my free, two-hour Laundry Camps that I run at the Mall of America in Minnesota, I share this philosophy with my campers—that caring for your loved ones' clothes shows them love. When their clothes are clean, smell wonderful, and look great, your loved ones are going to feel like they can take on the world, and their days are going to be all the brighter. That's true for you and your clothes as well. And don't you deserve that?

. . . .

My Beloved Granny Dude

More than anyone else in my life, Granny Dude (my mom's mom) helped grow my love of textiles. She appreciated beautiful clothes and relished the opportunity to buy them.

In fact, her sense of style had a profound impact on me—she was modern and fashion forward. And, as I look back, I realize her views on many issues were progressive, too.

A striking woman and always well turned out, as people used to say, she shunned a traditional bridal gown in 1949 (at age nineteen, no less) and instead wore an all-white suit, complete with tie and overcoat, which she purchased at Lazarus department store. I also know that to one funeral, back in the day, Granny Dude wore not a hat but a feather headband.

Obviously, this was a woman who knew herself, liked standing out, and didn't care what other people thought. In short, she was the perfect role model for a budding snappy dresser such as myself. In my teens, our shared love of clothing—and each other—brought us together for regular Thursday night Chinese dinners and evening shopping trips. We didn't always buy something, but we were always on the hunt.

Even when I was an adult, she loved treating me. Once, we were browsing in a Brooks Brothers store, and I couldn't decide which color gingham shirt to buy. Navy? Teal? Purple? Granny Dude announced that she'd solved the quandary: We'd get all six colors, and we did. She wasn't reckless with her money in general—only extravagant with regard to spoiling me.

I completely adored Granny Dude, and I know she felt the same about me. As an adult, I moved home for a year when my mom and Granny Dude were living together—I feel lucky to have had that time with her.

. . . .

Getting Started

Step one in your journey to keep your clothes from bossing you around is to be prepared. To begin transforming your laundry routine—and your textiles—you'll need to gather the supplies listed below. I know it's a long list, but don't worry: we'll break it down and cover everything in greater detail in later chapters. And I'll explain and make a case for each item as we go along.

Most of these items will last for at least a year, if not much longer, and many cost just a few bucks.

Supplies you will need:

- ☺ Soap flakes or a high-quality, plant-based liquid laundry soap that's free of petroleum, phosphate, phthalates, and parabens (if it contains any *p* words other than "*Patric*" or "*plant*," it's a no-go—and it also shouldn't have partificial, ahem, artificial colors)
- ☺ A bottle of bleach alternative (100 percent sodium percarbonate); when you're ready to use it, combine one tablespoon sodium percarbonate with one quart of water (this solution lasts roughly an hour—then it off-gases the extra oxygen molecule and the H_2O_2 becomes H_2O, or plain water)
- ☺ A box of washing soda (100 percent sodium carbonate)
- ☺ A small laundry brush (my favorite features horsehair)
- ☺ A laundry soap bar (used with the laundry brush for spot-cleaning and found at most grocery stores), such as Fels-Naptha
- ☺ A spray bottle that you've filled with 50 percent white vinegar and 50 percent water
- ☺ A store-bought bottle of 70 percent rubbing alcohol (isopropyl alcohol)
- ☺ A bottle of concentrated, oil-soap stain solution, such as The Laundress Stain Solution
- ☺ A small bottle of Amodex—magical, nontoxic

stuff recommended even by permanent-ink manufacturers

- ☺ A small spray bottle filled with cheap vodka (it's for
  your laundry, I promise)
- ☺ Laundry mesh bags in multiple sizes—but
  mostly small (get these online or from any
  big-box store)
- ☺ Inexpensive, white terry washcloths (I buy stacks
  of them)
- ☺ Cotton makeup pads
- ☺ A few safety pins (I use colorful diaper pins for a bit
  of whimsy)
- ☺ A new tube of tennis balls
- ☺ A yard of aluminum foil

For even more amazing laundry results and an extra dose of
fun, consider adding these:

- ☺ A small bottle or two of essential oils (peppermint and
  cinnamon are two of my favorites)
- ☺ Dye-trapping laundry sheets (I love these so much,
  and I am not paid to say so), such as Shout Color
  Catchers
- ☺ Three or more wool balls (sheep, llama, or alpaca
  wool—take your pick)
- ☺ A couple of bumpy rubber dryer balls (like the cute
  hedgehog ones)
- ☺ A drying rack
- ☺ Some tunes to groove to

☺ A disco ball hanging overhead (optional, but I think every laundry room needs one)

Supplies you *don't* need:

☺ Any popular detergent that comes in giant, multigallon bottles. Loaded with petrochemicals, this stuff is bad for your clothes, bad for your skin, and bad for the environment. Even "baby" and "free clear" laundry detergent has animal-based ingredients, plus chemicals such as sodium dodecylbenzenesulfonate, lauryl alcohol exothylate, sodium silicate, sodium xylenesulfonate, and stilbene disulfonic acid triazine derivative.

☺ Any popular detergent's colorful pods. They've got the chemicals mentioned above, but now they're in concentrated form. There's enough detergent in one pod to wash five loads of clothes—five loads! That means that many of these chemicals aren't washing away in the water but staying in your clothes. Plus, so many of these pods gunk up the sensors in washing machines that some Laundromats won't allow you to use them. They're also linked to allergies and skin rashes, and they're attractive dangers to candy-loving kids and adults with dementia. Have you seen the commercials, made by pod manufacturers themselves, devoted to educating people about keeping these pods out of reach from those who may not know better? I rest my case.

☺ More than two laundry baskets. I don't even use one. I toss my dirty clothes into a clothes hamper, which

I keep in my laundry room/master bathroom located just off my bedroom. Then, when I'm ready to wash, I simply throw the clothes into the machine. I find that I'm more likely to fold my clothes immediately if I don't have a laundry basket. (If yours has become more of a storage box for clean—or dirty—clothes rather than a container that transports clothes from bedroom to laundry room or Laundromat and back, you, too, may want to forgo laundry baskets.) That said, if your laundry room is more than a few steps away from your bedroom, investing in one or two easy-to-carry (and good-looking) laundry baskets or bags is perfectly acceptable.

- Fabric softener and dryer sheets. Don't even get me started on these two. (For seven reasons why you should never use either of these again, jump ahead to page 50.)

- Chlorine bleach and chlorine bleach pens. Do you know that most hospitals don't even use bleach for cleaning and disinfection anymore, and that the Environmental Protection Agency doesn't recommend bleach, even for black mold removal? Bleach irritates your eyes, nose, skin, and throat; damages equipment; and harms the environment. Enough said.

- Stain-removing sprays. These all-in-one options promise you stain-free textiles. But they often don't work. Why? Because specific ingredients remove specific stains. In other words, the elements that remove an organic oily stain, for example, will not remove an inorganic nonoily stain. Later in the book, I'll detail the three basic types of stains and how to remove all of them. Yes, really. Even the ones baked on in your dryer.

Let's Not Be Rash

Friends of mine (and Laundry Camp grads) were staying at a rented home on holiday and the entire family awoke the first morning covered by what appeared to be bedbug bites. They checked the mattresses, but no critters were found. However, an online search and quick visit to the laundry room revealed the likely culprit: detergent pods. Sure enough, their rashes matched the images they'd found online. So they stripped the beds and washed all the sheets and towels in warm water and baking soda—twice—and they alerted the homeowners to prevent this from happening to other guests. The lesson here: Washing your textiles with soap flakes or a safe, plant-based liquid laundry soap is not only good for your clothes, it is gentle on your skin.

OK, let's summarize:

- ☺ Now that you know to stop letting your clothes tell you what to do, your laundry routine is about to become simpler, faster, cheaper, and more fun!
- ☺ Your new, gentler laundry supplies will be kinder to your skin, your clothes, and the environment.
- ☺ You and your loved ones are going to be treated to softer and cleaner clothes, towels, bedding, and more.
- ☺ You'll be able to show love to the ones you love through the simple act of laundry.

Now that we've covered the key goals and basic supplies, it's time to sort!

2

It's Time to Sort It All Out

We should all do what, in the long run, gives us joy, even if it is only picking grapes or sorting the laundry.

—E. B. WHITE, AUTHOR

You know those funny posts featuring matchy-matchy family photos? Everyone is dressed identically, in T-shirts or tuxes, costumes or camouflage, even *Star Trek* uniforms.

That was not my family. Look at any Richardson family photo and it's a visual Crayola box: We're dressed in scarlet, goldenrod, shamrock, thistle. My family loves color. Especially my mom, who is at her happiest dressed in riotous shades. She stands out beautifully in any room. (I'm so proud of her: When I was in high school, Mom returned to college and reinvented herself. Strong and resilient in every way, she is the ultimate hostess and the queen of graciousness.)

I've always loved color, too. So I've never minded sorting clothes. I remember being a kid, kneeling on the floor, throwing item after item on the growing mounds of sorted colors that surrounded me.

While some families spent their weekends hiking the Appalachian Trail or watching their little soccer stars, my family shopped. At least Mom and I did. Dad, not so much, and the shopping gene skipped my brother. But Mom would even let me play hooky from time to time for special buying trips. In fact, for many years on my birthday, Mom, Granny Dude, and I would head north for a daylong shopping adventure at Lazarus department store in Columbus, Ohio. And all that shopping added up to a lot of colorful clothes.

The only problem? Washing clothes wasn't an everyday chore at my house. Today we don't think twice about throwing in a load of clothes anytime, any day of the week. Six a.m. before the kids wake up. Or at midnight when we want to watch the end of *Breakfast at Tiffany's* one more time.

But back then, people generally stuck to one major chore each day. Like the old nursery rhyme said: *Wash on Monday. Iron on Tuesday. Mend on Wednesday. Churn on Thursday.*[1]

---

1 One very old version of this rhyme says, "Brew on Thursday." I guess that was just their way of getting the weekend started early!

Clean on Friday. Bake on Saturday. Rest on Sunday. The idea of washing on Monday gave you lots of time to get everything dried, pressed, mended, etc. before the all-important Sunday church service at which you needed to look your best.

Even further back in time, for hundreds of years in Europe and maybe elsewhere, washing clothes once a month, or even less frequently, was often a sign of wealth—proving you had so many clothes and linens that you didn't need to launder more often than that. (Wealthy royals were even known to send their clothes off to professional launderers in Belgium.) In the meantime, people aired out clothes that had been worn but weren't actually dirty—a time-saving and Earth-friendly practice we should all consider taking up again.

But I digress. As a kid, washing once a week didn't help me when I wanted to wear my favorite duds more often. So I sometimes appealed to Granny Dude, who was only too happy to launder the clothes of her darling grandson. Eventually, I asked her to teach me how to wash my own clothes, which meant I could wear my current faves whenever I liked.

Mom made a deal with me: I could wash my clothes any day of the week, but I had to make it a full load, not just throw in the couple of items I wanted clean. That sounded fair. But before I could do that, I needed to learn how to sort. So Mom taught me the drill on sorting: whites, lights, and darks. Chances are you were taught to sort that way as well. And that advice served most of us pretty well in the decades leading up to the 1980s. But that wisdom has been flat wrong for *forty years* now!

How the Whites-Lights-Darks
Sorting Method Became a Thing

We think laundry takes oodles of time today. But it's nothing compared to washing back in the day (especially once you adopt my
methods). And I'm not even talking about pounding dirty clothes
on rocks in a stream or scrubbing them with a bar of soap on a
wooden washboard—which, as you can likely guess, is extremely
hard on clothes. Instead, I'm referring to using a wringer washer,
that groundbreaking invention from the mid-1800s that was electri-
fied at the turn of the last century.

Wringer washers provided one of the old-fashioned washing
methods that help explain whites-lights-darks sorting—clothes
needed to be separated when dyes bled more easily before advances
in textile technology. Granny Martha, on my dad's side, used just
such a machine until it stopped working and she could no longer
replace it. As a kid, I used to watch her launder all of her and Grandpa's clothes through the following steps:

- First, Granny Martha would fill her open-topped wringer
  washer about half-full with ten or so gallons of hot water.
  Then she'd add her detergent, likely Dash or Fab, and turn
  on the agitator. This rocket-shaped machine part, complete with fins and located at the washer's center, quickly
  turned clockwise and then counterclockwise, moving the
  clothes around in the soapy water. (Want to see a video?
  There are lots online.)
- Next, she'd place all the white clothes into the washer—
  that's because the water was at its cleanest at the start,

with no dirt and no dye. As each item became clean, she'd remove it from the washer, carefully and manually crank it through the attached wringer to remove the soapy water, and then place it in a dedicated laundry basket—one each for whites, lights, and darks. (This, by the way, is where we get the expression "to be put through the wringer," which refers to suffering from something terrible.)

- Granny Martha would then repeat this sluggish and laborious process next with the lights and, finally, with the darks—again, one item at a time. Meanwhile, the water would become increasingly dirty and dyed (from yesteryear's less-colorfast pigments).

- Once all the clothes had been washed and wrung out in that order—whites, lights, and darks—she'd pump out the now dirty water and replace it with clean water for rinsing.

- Then she'd start all over, this time with washed white clothes, rinsing and then wringing each item again, one at a time, until it was as dry as possible. These clothes were still wet and heavy, however—not nearly as dry as those that come out of our modern washing machines that boast fast spin cycles.

- Just prior to hanging up the whites to dry on her clothesline, Granny Martha would dump the lights into the tub for rinsing. Then, after hanging up the whites, she'd return to the washer to ring out the lights and then hang them up as the darks rinsed. Finally, she'd wring out the darks and hang them up to dry.

- Lastly, a few hours later, she'd return to the clothesline to take them all down, fold the items as she unclipped them, and then carry the clothesbaskets back into the house.

Land's sake—what a lot of physical work! No wonder our grandmas and great-grandmas only performed this half-day chore once a week. Otherwise they'd be doing laundry till the cows came home.

We can see from this step-by-step method why there's no reason to sort our clothes the whites-lights-darks way any longer, as our modern machines don't reuse the same wash or rinse water over and over again. Lucky for us, we can wash our clothes in any order we please.

. . . .

It was around the 1980s that manufacturers began outfitting washing machines with some pretty impressive technology that enabled us to wash larger loads at a quicker pace. In addition, dyes were becoming much more *fast*—*colorfastness* means that dye is resistant to fading or changing, thus making red-sock syndrome nearly a thing of the past.

Yet we were still following the old rules. No one, not even the manufacturers, taught us differently, so we continued sorting our clothes just like our parents and grandparents did back in the day, into whites, lights, and darks.

Until now. I'm here to teach you a faster, better way to sort, which will lead to a faster, better way to wash (we'll cover that in the next chapter). To avoid spending more time on laundry than needed, it all begins with sorting my way (cue Frank Sinatra).

By the end of this quick process, you'll have four (or possibly five) piles of textiles.

I know, I know: You're saying, "What do you mean *four* piles?! You just promised to make doing laundry smarter, easier, faster. But now we've got more piles?"

Yep. It's kind of like that old adage, "You don't get anything clean without getting something else dirty." Only in this case, you're going to get everything clean—with amazing results and in far less time. And, after all, few people only wash a white load, a light load, and a dark load every week. It's more likely they're doing all those, plus running separate loads of towels and lingerie and bedding. In fact—according to myriad sources, including The Spruce—the average American family does eight to ten loads of laundry per week. (Not to mention all the clothes they take to the dry cleaner.) Well, all that ends now.

First, walk through your house and gather up all your textiles—kitchen towels, bed linens, bath towels and rugs, throws and blankets, really anything that needs washing, plus everything from your laundry hampers. Then choose a spot in your house where you have lots of room to create piles. (For this step, it helps to have your laundry mesh bags and a few safety pins handy.)

Now let's get sorting:

1. Toss all your **whites** into one pile. We're talking white button-down shirts, white bras, white socks, white sheets, white towels, white elephants, etc. They all get thrown into this pile. So do all of your mostly white items with a bit of color—say, your white blouse with blue polka dots and your white pants with skinny black stripes. You'll also throw into this pile all your whiter-shade-of-pale clothes: off-white, cream, oatmeal, and

beige. Finally, if you have any items of the lightest lemon yellow, they belong in this pile, too.

2. Next, make a pile of all your **black clothes.** After all, we're living in the twenty-first century and we love our black clothes. Toss your black satin sheets into this pile, too—at least I do.

3. Colorfastness in textiles today allows us to change up our loads. For example, we no longer need to worry about purple dye leaking onto a blue shirt. So, the third pile is a pretty one made up of **cool colors:** blues, greens, and purples. Grays go into this pile, too. Again, we're talking your favorite blue jeans, your lacy purple bra, your green floral towels, your kid's navy pirate sheets—all your cool textiles.

4. Same goes for the fourth load, which is an equally lovely lump of **warm colors:** reds, yellows, browns, and oranges. This pile, too, includes a wide variety of items—your yellow chiffon dress, your coral towels, your spouse's khakis, your kid's hot-pink tutu—all your warm textiles.

Personally, I only wash my warm-colored clothes once every two weeks. I own so few warm-colored clothes that I actually bought red plaid boxers just to help make a full pile. (TMI?) Anyway, if you don't have enough textiles in one particular pile to garner a wash, skip that load this week. You have my permission. Or if you *really* need a particular garment washed this week but don't have enough similarly colored items, just handwash it. (See all my handwashing how-tos in the next chapter.) The reasons behind sorting the cool colors from the warm colors (no, you shouldn't wash them together) are these: If a microdye bleed occurs in the wash of either of these loads, no one will even notice. But if you mix cool colors with warm colors, a micro blue bleed, for example, might dot a red button-down with purple or a yellow T-shirt with green. In addition, due to their greater amount of dye, cool-colored clothes tend to be heavier than warm-colored clothes, and that means lots of abrasion if mixed together in a wash load—for example, your blue jeans sloshing around in a wash will be hard on your orange polo shirt. Don't do it. Your wash results won't be nearly as wonderful, and your clothes will wear out much faster.

That said, it *can* be confusing to determine what goes in which pile when it comes to our multicolored, multipatterned clothing. For more on what to do in those instances, see the sidebar that follows this section.

5. Finally, if you own **tech-driven, high-performance activewear**, you need one more pile. Think polypropylene, spandex, and other such high-tech fabrics included in workout wear by such brands as Athleta, Lululemon, Nike, Under Armour, etc. Throw your polyfleece into this pile, too.

Why does athletic gear get its own pile? It's because all of these activewear fabrics, in any color, are both hydrophobic and oleophilic. In other words, they hate water and love oil. That means they're extra thirsty when it comes to soaking up sweat and body oils, hanging on to them tightly throughout a wash cycle, such that water does nothing to eliminate the oil. That's why the more you work out in these clothes, the more they stink—whether or not you wash them. In addition, the sagging elastic in your swimwear hasn't lost its give; it's just bogged down by oil.

To get these clothes really clean and smelling good, you need a detergent that includes hydrogen peroxide, an enzyme that whisks away the oil. (I'll also point out that there's no law that says you *have* to work out in these clothes. Lounging around in them is perfectly acceptable.)

. . . .

The Gray Area

A few years ago, I was back home in Kentucky, holding a Laundry Camp for my mom and a bunch of her friends, who were all complete aces at the whites-lights-darks method. But my new sorting approach was throwing them for a loop.

"Where does my pink top with the blue floral print go?"

"I've got gray slacks with red pinstripes. Which pile do they go into?"

"What about my yellow polka-dotted navy blouse?"

"And my Lilly Pulitzer dresses?!" (They're Southern women, after all.)

No worries, I explained. Just choose the pile—cool colors or warm colors—that you think matches each item best. Still not sure? Look at the item from a bit of a distance and you'll see which color speaks most loudly to you. Same goes for argyles and ikats, paisleys and plaids. Don't stress about this—pick your pile and then get washing.

Well, Isn't That Special?

While the sorting plan calls for four piles (or five if you own high-tech workout gear), sometimes a week will deliver an extra load of wash. Say your family takes a camping vacation. You return home and everyone is invited (ordered) to bring their dirty, stinky hiking gear to the laundry room for an immediate wash. Or maybe it's a load of your child's (again, smelly) basketball gear. Or perhaps your pile of cool-colored clothes includes a dozen jeans of all sizes, so you dedicate an entire wash to dungarees. It happens—laundry doesn't follow strict rules all the time, and it's OK to change things up when life demands it.

My favorite special load is the Thanksgiving dinner linens back home in Kentucky. After cleaning up the dishes and tucking the leftovers into our second refrigerator on the back porch, it's time to do this bonus wash.

Prior to their washing, our vintage napkins, table runners, and tablecloths—some family heirlooms and some picked up at estate or rummage sales—could easily divulge, via their stains, what we enjoyed at our annual, colossal spread: the turkey, of course—a regal plumper baked to perfection and served with gravy—plus mashed potatoes, Louise's sweet potatoes, Granny Jiles's Sweet Potato Balls (recipe, page 170), corn, green beans, peas, brussels sprouts, cranberries (both relish and jelly), apple stack cake, red velvet cake, family friend Arlene's Sour Cream Pound Cake (recipe, page 171), my mom's Legendary Pumpkin Roll (recipe, page 172), and Maxine's Punch (recipe, page 167). I'm sure I'm forgetting something, but just writing this list makes my mouth water.

Whatever your extra load is, it's likely going to be personal. And don't sweat it—as in life, we all have extra loads to carry now and then.

Like my family's Thanksgiving linens or your hiking clothes from that woodsy vacation, the extra load just may be a sign of a life well lived. Do what you need to do, get 'em clean, and move boldly forward.

. . . .

Still with me? Good. Now that you've sorted, you'll need to do one more thing before washing: Gather up any wool and silk items from your piles. For each silky item (actual silk or fabric that just feels like silk), turn it inside out and place it into a mesh bag, one item per bag if possible. If your mesh bag is too big for your item, fold the bag down smaller and fasten the mesh with two or three safety pins.

Wool items are treated a bit differently to avoid felting. Now, I can imagine that you're concerned about washing wool. But don't fret: Follow the instructions in this chapter on how to prep woolen items for washing, and the next chapter for the washing itself, and all your wool items will come out clean, smelling great, and the same size they were before washing. And as a bonus, you won't go into shock over a dry cleaning bill.

Let's take one of your wool sweaters as an example.

Perhaps you inadvertently throw that wool sweater into the wash. It swims around in the washing machine and rubs against itself and other clothes. While it doesn't actually shrink, it does felt or matt like a dog's fur or hair (think dreadlocks), and emerges smaller. Now perhaps you didn't even realize that the sweater was in the wash and you throw it, along with the rest of that load, into the dryer. By the time your dryer *ding*s, you've got a sweater only a toddler could wear.

This is what happens to wool if washed and dried like other

clothes. We're going to take a completely different approach that avoids abrasion, leverages a short wash cycle, and eliminates the dryer—and it all starts with a special way of preparing your wool garments during the sorting process.

First, fold your sweater, just like you're going to be tucking it into a dresser drawer, then tightly roll it up, and place it into a mesh bag. If your mesh bag is too big for your sweater, like most of mine are, fold the bag snugly over the sweater and fasten the mesh securely with two or three safety pins. Each wool item should be stuffed as tightly as a giant sausage, with a mesh bag as its casing.

(Pro tip: Unless it's the victim of a spill, a wool sweater only needs to be washed once or twice a season. If a sweater smells, just air it out. Washing it rarely will not only save water and energy, but your favorite sweaters will last much longer!)

Continue placing all of your wool and silk items into mesh bags, and then return each to the proper color pile (we'll cover the washing part in the next chapter, but this is how to set yourself up for success during the sorting process).

Let's review:

- ☺ Gather up all of your textiles—clothes, sheets, towels, etc.
- ☺ Sort all of your textiles into piles: whites, blacks, cool colors, warm colors, and activewear if needed.

☺ Remove silky and wool items from each of these piles. Turn each silky item inside out, place each into its own mesh bag, and fasten with safety pins if needed. Ensure that each wool item is rolled up tightly, place each into its own mesh bag, and snugly secure each bag with safety pins.

☺ Return silky and wool items to their original piles.

Now that all of your piles are prepared, let the washing begin!

3

It'll All Come Out in the Wash

I feel that if I can do this, you know, if I can actually
do my own laundry, there isn't anything I can't do.
—JENNIFER ANISTON
AS RACHEL GREEN IN *FRIENDS*

You've likely washed countless loads of laundry in your life-
time. In Kentuckyspeak (and elsewhere, I'm certain), this isn't
your first rodeo. But perhaps you're having a hard time imagin-
ing that a new approach to washing your clothes will reinvent
your laundry experience. I can't wait to introduce you to this
fresh start—after all, laundry is really fun when you bring ex-
pertise and the right tools to the task.

Or perhaps doing laundry is mostly new to you. Maybe this book is a graduation present and you're headed off to college or life out on your own. Well, kudos! It's the perfect time to pick up these new skills.

As I mentioned before, I've been doing laundry since I was a wee lad, but as I matured, so did my skills—mostly through exploration and experimentation. Case in point: I didn't figure out how to machine-wash wool items until roughly a decade ago. And while I knew laundering basics in childhood (thanks, Mom and Granny Dude), my knowledge got a renewed kick-start when I entered the University of Kentucky as a freshman, studying merchandising, apparel, and textiles.

Away from home for the first time, I discovered that dry cleaning my wool sweaters, wool pants, and even wool Bermuda shorts was an expensive endeavor. *Who knew?* Well, my parents, of course—they'd been footing the bill. But I'd been clueless, since previously I'd just tossed my wool clothes into our dry-cleaning bag and they'd magically reappear, freshly cleaned and pressed, a week later. So I was facing a quandary: On a college-student budget, how could I, a dry-clean-only clotheshorse, wear clean clothes *and* still afford to eat?

I got a hint of the answer when Professor Kim Spillman opened my eyes to fashion as a global enterprise. We were studying gorgeously embroidered, traditional woolen textiles like *djellabas* from North Africa at the time, and a question occurred to me: Dry cleaning was invented in the 1800s, so how did people clean their wool clothing prior to that? Did other cleaning methods exist? And if so, what were they?

Not long after, a teaching assistant and I were paging through a J.Crew catalog and I was complaining about some dry-clean-only clothes that I liked but couldn't buy—I just couldn't afford to dole out any more money on dry cleaning. She confirmed my earlier thought that I likely didn't need to dry clean all my wool clothes, and she suggested that I approach another professor, Dr. Elizabeth Easter, with my question. Sure enough, Dr. Easter, an expert on textiles and their care, assured me I could handwash my woolens and then lay them flat to dry. She also noted that doing so was *preferable* for many articles of clothing, especially vintage and couture textiles.

Of course, handwashing wool makes perfect sense. After all, people didn't dream up wool clothing only after the invention of dry cleaning. In Europe, they've been wearing Scottish kilts, British jumpers (or sweaters), and Norwegian *bunads* for centuries. In the Middle East, Tunisians wore *chachias* and Algerians donned *gandoras*; in Asia, Mongolians pulled on *deels*; and in South America, there were Colombian ponchos, Chilean *chamantos*, and Peruvian *polleras*. Eventually I learned archeologists had discovered woolen clothing remnants that were thousands of years old. The oldest woolen garment ever found? A three-thousand-year-old pair of Chinese pants.

And so, thanks to Dr. Easter's advice, I was able to both wear clean woolens and support my thrice-daily habit of eating. Moreover, her counsel granted me a new freedom—to start exploring alternative ways to care for textiles.

Professor Ketch was important in this regard as well. She introduced me to haute couture, or high fashion, with a walk down the hall to the University of Kentucky's Betty D. Eastin Historic Costume Collection. Included in this collection are several items once owned by Kentucky-born Mona Williams—better known as the Countess Mona von Bismarck, and the first American ever voted, way back in 1933, "the best-dressed woman in the world." (I was so taken with her and her fashions, in fact, that years later I named my vintage clothing store Mona Williams in her honor.)

Among Bismarck's special items were a 1964 cream wool suit; a 1966 apricot-and-silver lamé frock; and a 1967 drop-dead-gorgeous, beaded-and-sequined, black silk gazar dress with matching cape. All were created by Cristóbal Balenciaga, famed Spanish Basque fashion designer, for his muse, Bismarck. And we, as lucky UK students, learned how to care for them. Getting to see, and sometimes touch, this finery and understand how each item was constructed had a profound impact on me.

The methods I learned at UK and have honed over the years—while working for many high-end department stores, including Neiman Marcus and Nordstrom, and assisting countless customers—can be applied to all of our clothes. Whether I'm washing a cashmere cardigan or my Culture Club T-shirt, I give them both gentle care. After all, I want to ensure they both last as long as possible. Don't your clothes deserve the same?

You're already on your way: You know a smarter way to sort, plus you understand how to care for silk and wool items before placing them into your washing machine. Now it's time to adopt new products and ways to launder.

Stinky Goats, Cashmere, and Your Washing Machine

When I introduce the idea of washing wool suits, cashmere scarves, mohair sweaters, and other such high-end items to my Laundry Campers, they're shocked!

But then I remind them that these incredibly fine, soft fabrics are derived from the coats of farm (and wild) animals, which aren't taking milk baths and eating bonbons all day.

Cashmere goats, for example, live mostly in the mountains of Asia. These goats are generally brown or gray (while some cashmere goats are somewhat white, only a precious few are entirely white—that's why, if you own white cashmere, it's likely been dyed), plus they're dirty and muddy. Boy goats, known as bucks or billy goats, have the added characteristic of being incredibly smelly. (Their strong urine scent works like magic on girl goats.)

More important to our understanding of caring for the resulting luxe fabrics is the fact that goats and sheep aren't rushed into barns at the first sign of inclement weather. Rain or snow? Bring it on.

Back when I worked at Neiman Marcus, a representative from Loro Piana, the preeminent cashmere brand, visited our store. She came all the way from Italy, because we were fortunate enough to have customers who had the desire and the ability to buy Loro Piana luxury sweaters, capes, scarves, and more—all items that included "dry-clean-only" tags. Yet during her presentation, she asked who among our team members washed their cashmere.

I was the only one who sheepishly (pun intended) raised my hand. "Now, that's someone who knows how to care for cashmere," she announced. Not only did she recommend washing, she noted that dry cleaning chemicals were far too harsh to use on cashmere. That's also true for mohair. (So why the "dry-clean-only" tags then? Most manufacturers worry that consumers may inappropriately machine-wash a garment and damage it.)

In addition, you rarely have to wash these fabrics unless an item is actually dirty. Until then, just air out these articles of clothing. And if an item has picked up the smell of cigarette smoke or smells like your favorite Thai restaurant, just spritz it lightly with straight vodka and the smell will disappear (someone alert the billy goats!).

Now you, too, know how to take care of these fabrics—it just helps to remember where they came from!

- -

True Blue

You adore your brand-new jeans, but how can you maintain that deep gorgeous blue? Or maybe you want to keep the midnight black of your denim jacket? Or perhaps you want to prevent your light-wash jeans from fading even a jot more? Here's a simple how-to: Add one-quarter cup of salt to a sink or large bowl filled with hot water. Then place your denim item into the basin and leave overnight. The next day, simply wash and dry as normal, and your denim should permanently hold its color. Easy!

- -

Bursting Your Bubbles

In a later chapter you'll learn how to treat stains immediately, prior to throwing your garments into the wash. But first, we need to turn our attention to soap. Yes, soap.

You've heard that old advice about not eating things whose ingredients you can't spell, let alone pronounce. A similar rule applies to soap. The ingredient lists of most detergents are packed

full of undecipherable, nearly impossible-to-spell chemicals—
many of which are harmful to your clothes, your health, and the
environment.

The toxicity of these chemicals hurts us daily in myriad ways,
the least of which is by wearing out our clothes far more quickly
than we'd like. One of the worst ways they harm us is with their
fragrance: When we smell the "fresh scent" of detergents, fabric
softeners, and laundry scent boosters (those beads you place in
the wash), we're actually breathing in volatile organic compounds
(VOCs), which are toxic chemicals that manufacturers, by law,
need not reveal. If you look on ingredient lists, you'll see that manufacturers take advantage of this and often only disclose categories
of ingredients—e.g., perfume dispersant, perfume, and dye—not
the actual ingredients themselves (any of which can be toxic).

According to the American Lung Association, "Breathing
VOCs can irritate the eyes, nose, and throat, can cause difficulty
breathing and nausea, and can damage the central nervous system as well as other organs. Some VOCs can cause cancer." In
addition, diethyl phthalate (DEP)—a dispersant, or common
element that spreads these fragrances—is a likely endocrine dis-
ruptor; that means that it may disturb hormone functions and
could damage reproductive and developmental processes.

Detergents can also include dangerous phenols—corrosive
and toxic acids. Easily absorbed by our skin, phenols can cause
serious health problems, including chemical blisters and burns,
organ damage, even death. In addition, some detergents include
toxic surfactants (a fancy word for detergents), which may cause
water pollution and affect aquatic organisms.

Studying all the gobbledygook chemical names and their toxicity can lead you down a bottomless research hole. Here's what

you really need to know: First, many big-name manufacturers use dangerous chemicals. Second, by law, they don't have to divulge every chemical used in their ingredient lists. And third, you can help protect yourself and your loved ones, not to mention the environment, by switching to soaps or detergents made with plant- and mineral-based ingredients, essential oils, and floral extracts.

The soap flakes I created and make available in my store, for example, are based on a two-hundred-year-old recipe from a New Zealander woolier. They use sunflower oil, food-grade lye, and coconut oil. That's it—just three ingredients. And none of them negatively affects your health or creates irritating manufactured smells. (I've never understood why our clothes have to smell like the tropics, or "twilight," or avocado; I like my cotton shirts to smell like, well, cotton.) These soap flakes work best when added right into your washer—top load or front load— with your clothes; don't place flakes in your washer's dispenser. In fact, I recommend doing the same with a safe, plant-based, liquid laundry soap, too.

You can find other safe, high-quality detergents out there as well. Check packages for such words as **nontoxic, biodegradable, allergen free, bleach free, petroleum free, phosphate free,** and **phthalate free.** And check for a shorter list of ingredients that you recognize. Then you'll know you're on the right track. As a bonus, most of these better detergents require far less product— much like washing your hair with an expensive shampoo versus a discount shampoo. For example, while a big-name brand may call for a quarter cup or even a half cup of detergent per load, higher-quality laundry soap may require only a single tablespoon.

Moreover, it's not the soap that truly gets your clothes clean— it's the water. The soap just lowers the viscosity of the water molecules, or in other words, it makes the water wetter. This allows the water to slide right through your clothes, removing dirt, oil, and more. This is yet another reason we don't need big-name detergents with their long lists of chemical ingredients. Instead, use far less of a high-quality soap, and not only will your clothes look and feel better, so will you.

. . . .

The Big White Lie

I've already mentioned that you should put the kibosh on using chlorine bleach, or sodium hypochlorite, for its inherent health risks. But I'm guessing you might not be convinced. After all, you want white whites—glowing T-shirts, radiant button-downs, I-need-my-sunglasses towels. But what if I told you that your chlorine bleach is actually causing your whites to yellow? Well, it's true.

When you buy amazingly white textiles, it's because they've been treated with optic white dye. That is not the natural color of cotton. So the first time you add chlorine bleach to a load of towels, for example, the towels won't show much fading. But the second time you wash them with added bleach, you're actually starting to bleach away that white color, turning the cotton back to its original ecru color. The third time you wash with bleach, you've just kissed that white goodbye. And now you're probably adding extra bleach, thinking that will solve the problem—but it's only making it worse.

So how do you keep your whites white? First, don't ever wash with chlorine bleach. Second, to maintain your textiles' white dye, wash your whites with a gentle soap and a tablespoon of chlorine-free oxygen bleach. This nontoxic, biodegradable bleach alternative, also known as sodium percarbonate, will whiten your clothes safely and beautifully. One caveat: Don't use it for washing silks or woolens.

. . . .

Washing Whites One Hundred Years Ago

At the turn of the last century, students learning about laundering at the Teachers College of Columbia University were taught by Lydia Ray Balderston, arguably the foremost laundering expert at the time. This professor wrote several volumes on the subject, including *Housekeeping Workbook, Housewifery,* and *Laundry Manual.* From her book entitled *Laundering,* published in 1914, she offered the below thirteen steps to caring for white clothes. This list makes me grateful for technology.

1. Soaking
2. Washing
3. Rinsing
4. Boiling
5. Rinsing (again)
6. Bluing
7. Starching
8. Hanging
9. Drying
10. Sprinkling
11. Stretching
12. Ironing
13. Folding

. . . .

All Washed Up

When it comes to washing, we also need to consider our washing machines and how we use them. As I mentioned before, washing machine technology has advanced impressively over the years. Have you checked out the control panel of a high-tech washing machine lately? There are enough dials, buttons, and lights to rival an airplane dashboard. Despite that, most of us continue to wash our textiles the same way we did before these fancy new machines. More's the pity. After all, we don't still use iceboxes and telephone party lines.

Actually, the telephone makes a great analogy. At the turn of the last century, switchboard operators connected neighbors to one another via party lines. (And nothing but a clear conscience stopped busybodies from listening in on one another's conversations.) Eventually, individual lines offered improved privacy. And technology continued to move forward with the dial phone, the push-button phone, the cordless phone, and then a series of mobile phones: the "brick," dubbed for its weight and size; the "bag," nicknamed for its carrying case; the razor; the beloved flip (I still miss mine); the ever-smaller and thinner mobile; and, finally, the computer in our pockets—most especially, the iPhone and the Android. Who knows what telephonic advance will be next?

With each improvement, we've had to pick up new skills— how to place a phone call, how to take photos, how to text, how to use apps, etc. And if Apple or Verizon didn't teach us, a member of the younger set was only too happy to explain better, faster ways of doing things.

But this could not be further from our experience with washing machines. While the technology has advanced ever forward, no one has taught us how to get the most out of our machines. That is, until now.

In actuality, most of the technology is built right into your washing machine. In other words, you rarely need to use all the bells and whistles that your machine settings boast. Nope, for nearly every single wash, you'll need to do just two things.

First, wash everything—and I do mean everything—on warm. Yes, your darks. Yes, even your delicates. *But what if I use a detergent designed for cold water?* you ask. It doesn't matter—warm, warm, warm.

The thing is, even cold-water detergents are designed to work in water that's 58 to 62 degrees Fahrenheit; manufacturers define this as cold. Unfortunately, cold water in our homes is likely just 53 or so degrees. And that means our cold-water setting isn't warm enough to dissolve our detergents—which means they're not activating and our clothes aren't getting clean.

Want proof? Find an item you've recently washed in cold water and throw it into truly warm water—it will suds right up. *That's because the soap is still in your clothing.* And I hate to say it, but that means all the dirt and sweat and who knows what else is, as well. *Ew.* So crank up the warm. (Do your towels smell sour despite being washed? Cold water is likely why. Most Laundry Campers who've been using cold-water detergents and settings tell me that a pile of towels is the first load they'll be washing in warm when they get home.)

And don't worry—warm water will not fade or shrink your clothes. Most wash cycles include four steps: the wash, the rest, the rinse, and the spin. Only the wash stage uses warm water, meaning that your clothes will only be in warm water for eight or so minutes, just long enough to get them clean but never so long as to do them harm.

Which leads me to the second thing you'll be doing with each wash: You're going to wash everything on the express cycle, sometimes called the fast, quick, or super-speed cycle. Running for a total of roughly twenty-eight minutes, depending on your machine, the express cycle takes your clothes through an eight-minute wash and an eight-minute rinse (plus the rest and the spin)—plenty of time to get your clothes clean.

This short cycle is much kinder to your clothes than a full cycle, helping them last longer since we're no longer prolonging the time they're exposed to soap, water, and other clothes. After all, most of us are not cleaning sewers, mining coal, or having paintball fights. We're just living our lives and getting the odd bit of mustard or drip of Diet Coke on our shirts now and then (or every day, in my case). The express wash delivers great results—and saves you lots of time and water.

Most important, I highly encourage washing all of your textiles in a single day, preferably the same day each week. Doing so will mean that you'll have all of your clothing ready and available to you the other six days of the week. Getting all the wash done in a single day also feels great—you won't constantly feel like you have to throw in another load of wash. This experience can be revelatory: imagine not feeling a daily pressure to clean your clothes, knowing that your laundry can wait for its assigned day of the week. (Imagine, too, if we treated our work in the same way—not letting it spill into our days off—how awesome would that be?)

Understanding the Bells and Whistles

While the express wash is always my first choice, let's get to know the pros and cons of your washing machine's other cycles:

- Delicates (or Handwashing) generally uses cold water, which, as you now know, isn't likely to clean your garments. In addition, this cycle uses a slow spin, which means more abrasion (even in mesh bags), more lint, and less-than-ideal cleaning results.
- Permanent Press, one of the newer wash cycles, historically, is meant to minimize wrinkles. It uses a warm wash and a cold rinse—both good features—but a slower spin than I prefer. If you can select the length of the wash on this one, go for the eight-minute cycle. If you can't, stick with the express wash. One more thing to consider: Your clothes emerge a little wetter in this cycle than in others; the idea is that when you then throw these items in the dryer, more steam will be generated for fewer wrinkles.
- Cottons (or Normal) uses warm water and a cold rinse. The drawback of this cycle is that it runs too long. Your clothes just don't need to become that familiar with the inside of your washing machine.
- The idea behind Whitest Whites is to beat the devil out of your towels. It's a really long setting, it uses hot water, and its action is extra aggressive. Thank you but no, no, and no.
- Meant for kids' clothes or undergarments, Sanitary (or Sport) is about the same as Whitest Whites but uses extra

hot water to kill bacteria. Your clothes just don't need this, though. When we wash our hands with soap and warm water, we know they're clean. There's no need to scald our hands to kill germs. The same holds true for our clothes.

- If you're using the right amount of soap, you don't need the Extra Rinse; it also causes more abrasion. That said, if you use a pod, you can never use the Extra Rinse enough (think Hoover Dam).

. . . .

Now, remember those five piles of wash you prepared? It's time to get down to it. But before you do, here are a few last-but-not-least tips:

- Select High Spin for each of your loads; you want your textiles to be as dry as possible to shorten their time spent in your dryer and on your drying racks.
- If you have a stain you want to treat, skip ahead to Chapter 7 for the lowdown on stains before throwing that garment in the washing machine.
- If you really, *really* want to wash your towels in hot water, it's not my preference, but it's OK. Fabrics that can stand up to hot water are made of plant-based fibers, including cotton, linen, bamboo, and hemp. (Note: The threads holding your cotton towels together are likely polyester, so all that hot water isn't good for them.)
- If you've got a beaded item or one with sequins, be sure to turn it inside out and place it in a mesh bag so it doesn't snag other items.

☺ Consider adding a dye-trapping laundry sheet to each wash. This handy small sheet helps soak up stains, any microbleeding, and hard-water minerals during the wash cycle. Best of all, you don't need a full sheet. Simply rip a full one in half and toss half in.

☺ If you have a front-loading machine, don't worry about putting in an extra-large load. This can't be said for a top-loading machine, which generally has a higher tendency to become unbalanced and deliver an error message.

☺ If you have a load of really, *really* dirty clothes—for example, clothes you've worn hiking or gardening—add a quarter cup of washing soda, poured right on top of your clothes, to boost the cleaning power of the wash. The washing soda, or sodium carbonate (often sold in grocery stores—although it's not food safe), softens the water, allowing the detergent both to remove dirt from your textiles and keep the soil in the water, rather than redepositing it on the clothes.

Washing Your Washing Machine— and Your Dryer

Now that you're using better—and far less—soap, your washing machine will experience little product buildup and require less-frequent cleanings. That's especially true if you remember to leave your washing machine's door open whenever it's not in use. However, when your machine begins to smell, it's time to get cleaning. Simply pour one pound of Borax directly into your empty washing machine; turn on your hottest, longest cycle; and then pour a gallon of white vinegar in your dispenser. Done! Periodically, I also scrub the dispenser drawer with a fifty-fifty mixture of vinegar and water. As for cleaning your dryer, once it's cool, spray the inside with your fifty-fifty mixture of vinegar and water, and then wipe down with a clean, white terry washcloth.

· ·

One More Option: Handwashing

There are times when you may want to consider washing your garments by hand. Perhaps you've got just an item or two to wash of one category (e.g., whites or activewear)—not nearly enough for a full load. Or maybe you're sick and don't want to spread your germs among others, so a trip to the Laundromat is out of the question. Handwashing is a perfectly acceptable option, and it can get your clothes just as clean as machine washing as long as you follow the steps below.

To begin, I recommend using your kitchen sink; its generous size will accommodate a few items at a time yet not require the amount of water needed to fill, say, a bathtub for handwashing. First, clean your sink. Then fill it with warm water and add a smidgen of soap flakes, a few pumps of foaming hand soap, or a capful of mild shampoo. Don't use dish soap, as that's far too harsh, and laundry detergent isn't recommended, either, because it's so challenging to manually rinse out of clothes.

Next, add your clothes (be sure to maintain your categories—that is, whites, blacks, etc.) and gently manipulate them in the water with your fingers (don't wring or twist) every three to four minutes. After a total of twenty minutes, let the water drain, fill the sink with cool water, and then swish the clothes through the fresh water. Repeat this step one more time, letting the water drain, refilling with cool water, and moving the clothes through the water one more time. By now, the water should be nearly clear and your items should be clean. Briefly roll up the wet clothes in a towel to remove excess moisture or fling out excess water with a quick twirl in a clean salad spinner. Then hang up the items to dry on plastic hangers or a drying rack.

But what if you need to sanitize your clothing? Again, you're home sick, you're caring for someone who is, or perhaps someone in your family has a job that has contact with pathogens. While a washing machine uses heat to sanitize, in handwashing it's the lipids in the soap that glom on to germs and take them right down the drain with the water. So the handwashing method described above is all you need. That said, if you want to ensure your clothes are fully sanitized, you can steam them after washing with a steamer or a steam-generating iron; the steam well exceeds the 167 degrees Fahrenheit required to kill off flu viruses.

. . . .

Got the Blues?

Some things you just can't improve on. Ever since the 1880s, Mrs. Stewart's Bluing has been made right here in my adopted state of Minnesota. It's awesome, inexpensive, nontoxic, and biodegradable—made mostly of blue pigment and water. You can purchase bluing online or at a grocery or discount store.

Traditionally, homemakers would dribble a couple drops of

bluing into their wash water to bring back the original color in their white garments, sheets, and towels. That's because adding microscopic blue particles to white fabric causes it to reflect more light and look whiter. And we all love bright whites.

What's changed today is our washing machines. Most of us use high-efficiency, or HE, washing machines that use much less water than back in the day, which means that bluing is much less diluted. That's why I can't recommend using bluing except in a handwashing scenario—whether you want to whiten a special shirt, an heirloom tablecloth, or perhaps a vintage item you've just purchased.

Here's what you do: After washing or handwashing an item, add a few drops of bluing to a sink or washtub filled with tepid water. The water should look baby blue. Swish the item three or four times in the bluish water, and then let dry. To get the effect you want, you may need to repeat the process two or three times. Do not add more bluing to the water to try to get it done faster. Once you've successfully used bluing on a particular garment, you can wash it normally three or four times before needing to repeat the bluing process.

. . . .

Hopefully you're feeling great about these simple yet chore-shortening, energy-saving, and results-oriented changes to your laundry routine. When you're done with the washing, turn the page: It's time to level up the way you dry clothes.

4

The Good Kind of Dry Spell

There is joy in clean laundry. All is forgiven in water, sun, and air.

—RUTH MOOSE, EXCERPT
FROM POEM "LAUNDRY,"
POET AND NOVELIST

For decades now, my career in fashion has made me a matchmaker of sorts. Working at fine department stores like McAlpin's and Neiman Marcus, or my own boutique, Mona Williams, has meant introducing clients to amazing clothes they fall in love with. Depending on the client and the occasion, that may mean a dark navy jean and a colorful graphic tee topped by a camo jacket. Or it could be a jacquard sheath dress finished by a matching coat. Or, once in a while, it indicates a designer gown by, perhaps, Carolina Herrera, Badgley Mischka, or, more classically, Bill Blass or Coco Chanel. I've been a fan of luxury clothing, particularly vintage, since college.

But don't misunderstand. My personal idea of luxury isn't designer duds. It's not even *shopping* for clothes—although I do love a good shopping trip. My idea of the ultimate in luxury is sun-dried, fresh-smelling laundry taken right off the line—especially sheets, and then sleeping in those sheets. Sheer heaven.

Unfortunately, too few of us hang our clothes outside to dry these days. In roughly just a generation—whether it's our busy lives necessitating quicker options, the lack of outdoor space (let alone a backyard), or worry over our neighbors' opinions of a line full of clothes—hanging out the laundry has become a fading, if not nearly obsolete, practice in the United States. And that's a shame for lots of reasons.

One of my fondest childhood memories of Granny Dude was keeping her company as she hung up laundry in the bright sunshine. As a boy, it was my frequent duty to hand her laundry pins, or pegs, one by one as she pinned up the wash to dry. And I loved helping her, although I'm guessing that my presence underfoot actually made the chore last a bit longer.

Late in the afternoon, we'd return to the backyard, where she'd take down all the wash—the towels and sheets, neatly stretched along the line and crimped at each edge; the shirts and blouses, hung by their hems to avoid pin marks at the shoulders; the pants, usually pegged at their ankles for faster drying; and finally, the socks and underwear—boxers, panties, and bras. (Of course, she'd typically hang these more personal items between two rows of sheets.)

As Granny Dude would remove the laundry, starting with the largest items first, she'd fold each piece and then let it drop into the basket. And she'd end with the smallest items, typically socks, topping off the pile. I remember her enjoying the process, maybe the meditative quality of it, and so did I.

Yet even Granny Dude didn't always have the luxury of time. A progressive woman, she worked as a hygienist, then as an office manager, at a dentist's office. Her husband, my granddad, was a barge pilot, working thirty days on the Ohio and Mississippi rivers, and then enjoying thirty days off. Come to think of it, I don't ever remember spending languid laundry afternoons with her when he was home. My guess is that she treasured her time with him and took shortcuts with daily chores when he wasn't working on the barge. Perhaps in those periods she even used her dryer.

Three Drying Guidelines

That brings us back to the topic at hand: drying our clothes and textiles. When it comes to the actual process of drying, I follow three basic guidelines:

- 😊 I place anything woven—as in items made by weaving (with interlacing strands and filling threads)—on hangers; these include shirts, jackets, trousers, and overcoats.
- 😊 I hang all my knits—for example, sweaters—on a drying rack. (If your jeans have a bit of stretch, always hang them up to dry on pant hangers or a drying rack.)
- 😊 And I throw T-shirts, socks, underwear, sheets, and towels into the dryer.

I'm guessing you might be resistant to line-drying your clothes, thinking that doing so will be tedious and take much longer than just tossing them into the dryer. But laying them over a drying rack or placing them on hangers takes just a couple of minutes. Plus, these drying methods are great for your clothes and kind to the environment.

Still, you might not have time to hang up every load of your clothes. Maybe you've got a crazy busy day and a short amount of time to have everything washed, dried, folded, and put away. Or maybe you've got young kids who will outgrow their clothes long before their clothes wear out. So if need be, you can just fling your clothes into the dryer when necessary.

But you may want to consider line-drying your clothes as a goal to shoot for—say, once every other load, or every third load. Just think of the positive impact we'd have on the planet if all of us, even twice a month, hung up our clothes to dry!

Now let's talk further about my drying strategies and the reasons behind them:

First, most high-quality textiles can endure just fifty trips through the washer and dryer. That means if you machine wash and machine dry a favorite shirt once a week, you'll have worn it out in a year. If, however, you skip the dryer and hang up this item to dry, you've just bought yourself at least seventy more trips through the washer—and more than another year of wear, says the National Council of Textile Organizations. So those gingham shirts I love, or your personal favorites, will last that much longer if they're not tumbling around in a dryer every week. Plus, you'll save a bunch of money: You'll have used less electricity in drying and you won't have had to replace that item prematurely.

Second, you do NOT have to lay knits flat to dry. Consider this a reminder not to let your clothes boss you around. Before I knew better, I would cover my bedroom floor and my bed with sweaters drying atop clean towels. No more! If your wash cycle is set on fast spin, then your knits should come out of the washing machine barely damp. Just shake them out, pat out any wrinkles, and carefully drape them over your drying rack. They'll be dry in no time. (Pro tip: Just like with your wool sweaters, unless your knits have stains, you don't need to wash them more than once or twice a season. You can just air them out most of the time.)

Third, there are simple ways to care for the items you do put in the dryer. As I mentioned before, I dry all my T-shirts, socks, underwear, sheets, and towels in the dryer. That said, before I hit the "on" button, I tend to do the following:

- 😊 I toss in at least three wool balls, which reduce the time spent drying my clothes by up to forty percent. (Save the tennis balls for down items.) And if I'm feeling extra fancy, I add a couple drops of essential oil to the wool balls to scent my laundry. Alongside the sunshine and fresh air, scenting my sheets with cool peppermint helps make my summer nights extra restful. Peppermint also clears the head, so that I'm not dwelling on any worries from my day. And in the winter, I use lavender for relaxation or allspice for comfort.

- 😊 If I'm drying towels, I also toss in bumpy dryer balls, which help separate laundry as it's drying and plump up the terry cloth. Nowadays, you can even buy bumpy dryer balls that look like puffer fish, hedgehogs, and cacti—all with smiling faces.

- 😊 Finally, for one of my best-ever laundry tricks, I place a tightly rolled ball of aluminum foil in every dryer load to discharge any static from my laundry. Take a yard of aluminum foil and roll it into a ball, roughly the size of a baseball. Then just throw it into your dryer. It should last about sixty loads, getting increasingly smaller with each. Once it shrinks to the size of a golf ball, simply toss it into your recycling container and start over with a new ball of aluminum foil.

This leads me to . . .

Seven Things I Hate about Fabric Softeners and Dryer Sheets

You'll notice that I do not suggest using fabric softeners and dryer sheets. That's intentional: I hate them, and you should, too. In fact, I hate them more than squirrels and mosquitoes. I hope that you will never, ever use either of these products again for these seven reasons:

1. The first time you use fabric softener on a load of clothes, you're coating your textiles with silicone and cutting their absorbency by up to eighty percent. That means, for example, that your towels will no longer do what they were made to do—soak up water.
2. You're diminishing your clothes' breathability, coating the spaces between the yarns. So sure, a T-shirt may feel soft having been dried with fabric softener, but the

next time you wear it on a hot, sunny day, you might as well be wrapped in cellophane.

3. When you use dryer sheets or fabric softeners, stains become incredibly hard to remove. Whenever someone tells me that a stain-removal method doesn't work, my first guess as to the culprit is either dryer sheets or fabric softener, as both can create a silicone coating. Again, the silicone has coated the clothing and made the stain all the more difficult to extract from underneath it. Before you can eliminate the stain, you first have to get rid of the silicone.

4. The silicone also coats your dryer's lint catcher, which can help attract lint, which, in turn, can cause dryer fires. According to the U.S. Fire Administration, failure to clean out lint from clothes dryers accounts for thousands of house fires every year.

   Try this: Pull out your dryer's lint catcher and place it under a running faucet; if it holds water, that means it's coated in silicone and high time you clean it. Fill your sink with hot water and scrub the mesh with a bristle brush to remove the residue. Then, stop using dryer sheets or fabric softeners, and continue to remove lint from your dryer lint catcher after *every wash*.

5. Dryer sheets often include phthalates, known endocrine disrupters that can cause health problems for children, pregnant women, and their babies in utero. I'd say that's a very high price to pay to have your clothes smell like Ragweed Sunshine.

6. Some people recommend placing fabric sheets around

your home's foundation or in your boat to keep mice away. So here's my thought: If mice are smart enough to run away from fabric sheets, why aren't you, too? And why would you voluntarily rub them on your clothes if they can be used as an animal repellant?

7. Last but not least, if you're vegan (or even if you're not), you might shudder to learn that one of the main ingredients used in fabric softener and added to dryer sheets, dihydrogenated tallow dimethyl ammonium chloride, is derived from horse, cow, and sheep fat. So if you use fabric softener on your clothes, you're actually wearing Seattle Slew or Secretariat. *Ew.* And let's just say, that animal fat doesn't smell good. That's why they have to add the petrochemical fragrances in as well. How good does Jungle Rain smell to you now?

. . . .

Tackling Knits with Blocking

Need a knitted top, skirt, or pant taken in a pinch or let out a smidge? (Or maybe more than a smidge?) Then blocking is just what the tailor ordered. But there's no need to visit a professional. With a little practice, blocking is a helpful technique you can do at home—expanding your wardrobe options and making your clothes, and you, look all the better. It's a skill I use frequently for my customers and for myself. First I'll share the background and then all the details.

Long ago I learned how to block when I was working at Embry's department store. There, we sold lots of St. John knits, and being able to block, an age-old seamstress skill, gave me an edge when serving my customers. Let's say the waist of a sweater fit a customer perfectly, but the chest needed to be more generously sized, or the shoulders broader, or the sleeves longer. While my guest waited in the dressing room, I'd visit the store's steam table and customize the fit. That way she could go home with the garment in hand, rather than have to return days later to pick up the tailored item.

While blocking takes a bit of practice, here are the basic steps:

1. Before washing your garment, lay it flat and then measure its width and its length. Pay particular attention to the area you want to make larger or smaller. How much—an inch, two inches? Make note of that.

2. Wash as normal.

3. Lay the clean and damp garment flat again and massage the section of the garment with your hands to the size you require—based on the measurement you took previously.

4. To ensure the garment dries exactly to your preferred dimensions, I recommend pinning the item along its edge with straight pins every two inches. Then let it dry.

5. Once your garment is completely dry, remove the pins and it's ready to wear. This perfect fit should likely last through several washes and sometimes even longer.

. . . .

Game to Line-Dry Your Laundry?

During the weeks when you have time to avoid the dryer all together, there's always the option to line-dry your laundry. And did you know that hanging out the laundry can be courageous?

During four years of the Revolutionary War, it is believed that Long Island resident Anna Smith Strong served as a spy for the Culper Ring, which provided news of the British military's movements in New York City and Long Island to General Washington. This mother of nine cleverly signaled the arrival and whereabouts of another spy by hanging out a black petticoat and a varying number of handkerchiefs to dry. Who knew laundry could be so exciting? (Well, of course, I did—and now you do, too.)

If you want to be patriotic like Strong, or if you just want to go big and go outside for the freshest-smelling clothes and sheets ever, there are some simple techniques you can follow. And if it's freezing or raining outside, or if you don't have outdoor space, just bring the laundry show inside. Either way, your clothes will thank you, the Earth will thank you, and I'll thank you. (Thank you!)

To get started, use my clothesline tips:

☺ To begin, place similar, just-washed items together in your laundry basket, from smallest to largest: for example, first the underwear, then the shirts, then the towels, and, lastly, the sheets.

☺ Once outside, hang these similar items together, now largest to smallest—especially if you have a multiline clothesline, which allows for greater airflow and faster drying. (In other words, in this example, sheets are hung first, towels go on the next line, tops are clipped to the third line, and underwear goes on the last line.)

☺ To hang a flat sheet, fold it in half and then clip it to the clothesline along its hems; for a fitted sheet, fold in half and clip the sheet along its middle, tucking the elasticized corners inside one another—they hang at the bottom.

- To maximize clothesline space, overlap edges of flat items—say, towels—so that a single clothespin can crimp the corners of two towels.
- Hang white clothes and sheets during the sunniest time of day for the ultimate in sunshine brightening.
- For brightly colored T-shirts and tops, plus dark jeans, consider turning garments inside out before hanging to avoid fading.
- Hang shirts and blouses upside down, clipping at each side seam.
- Hang pants by their ankles and, if you have two lines, clip one pant leg to one line and one to another for faster drying—thanks to greater airflow.
- When all of your items are dry, remove them from the line, working largest to smallest again, beginning with sheets or towels.
- To save time, consider folding each item before you drop it into the basket.
- Know that, as with any task, you'll get faster as you get the hang of it. And really, once you do, it's easy!

Supplies you need:

- An outdoor clothesline or drying rack: Read reviews to find the best one for your space and needs. You can find large umbrella-shaped rotary dryers, collapsible dryers, and retractable single and multiple clotheslines.

- ☺ An indoor clothesline or drying rack: Again, check out the wide variety of indoor options available, including retractable clotheslines; wall-mounted stainless-steel racks; self-standing bamboo racks; and three-tier, rolling drying racks. No doubt there's an option that will suit your needs.
- ☺ A pack of fifty or one hundred clothespins.
- ☺ A canvas clothespin bag that hangs on your clothesline (you can find cute handmade ones online) or another container for your clothespins. You can even use a fanny pack with a large pocket.
- ☺ A fun hat, your favorite sunglasses, your sunblock (even a fifteen-minute clothesline session requires protecting your skin), and your fitness tracker (you'll be burning calories).
- ☺ Tunes to set the mood. Or skip the headphones and enjoy the outdoor sounds around you.

. . . .

Knocking Out Wrinkles with Your Dryer

To remove wrinkles from damp silk or silky items, you can throw them into the dryer on the lowest heat setting or no-heat setting for up to three minutes—and it works. I, however, never use this method, because I'm just not that focused.

In the past, I'd throw in a silk garment and get sidetracked, perhaps pulled in by a Hallmark Channel flick about a Calpurnian prince and a New York City girl. Suddenly ten minutes have flown by, my silk items have white streaks, and a few bad words have been said.

If you're more focused than I am, go ahead and toss in the silk items, but stay close by the dryer and grab those garments out after just a minute or two and then hang them up. (While you're waiting, why not juggle a few extra wool balls?)

. . . .

Airing Out Your Clothes

We launder our clothes far too much. Often we wash our clothes after a single wear, with not even the tiniest dot of dirt on them. Our excuse? They don't have that just-washed feel, they've lost their shape, or they smell—a bit. At this point, clothes don't need washing but instead simply an airing out and maybe a quick session with a steamer. For more on steaming, see page 66. In the meantime, let's focus on airing out, which is so much easier than washing, drying, and hanging or folding. Plus, it saves time and is better for the planet.

Here are my two favorite ways to air out clothes:

1. Place your strong-smelling clothes on hangers and then hang them outside for a few hours on a porch, deck, or laundry line. In a pinch, you can even hang them up in the garage. A friend of mine used to attend sales meetings where most of the sales reps smoked cigarettes. Once back home, she'd strip down to her underwear in her (attached) garage and hang up her clothes to air out.

2. When your clothes smell like smoke, French fries, or something else a bit off, you can use one of my favorite tricks—relied on by many professional costumers and hockey parents everywhere. I use this a lot, including after visits

to a local Thai restaurant whose coatrack is located right outside the kitchen. While I love Thai food, I don't want to smell like *kao klook gapi* when I get home.

So here's what you do: Simply pour vodka (cheap vodka works just as well as the fancy Belvedere) into a spray bottle and spritz on the article in question. The vodka kills any bacteria and removes all scents, including cigarette smoke and strong food odors. (This technique also works on carpets for pet smells and sanitizes cutting boards in the kitchen.)

One of my customers, a high school marching band director, offered up a challenge for me regarding this advice. While his band's uniforms began to smell after just one or two halftime shows, he couldn't afford to dry clean them regularly, but he also couldn't keep bottles of vodka at school. No worries, I told him. Simply add a tablespoon of rubbing alcohol to each spray bottle of vodka to make it denatured, or undrinkable. Adding the rubbing alcohol to the vodka is a good method, too, for anyone who—for whatever reason (a religious objection, a recovering family member, etc.)—doesn't want alcohol in his or her home. As a bonus, stir in a few drops of an essential oil for a great scent. Problem solved!

Let's review:

- ☺ To dry your garments, hang your woven items on hangers, hang your knits on a drying rack or clothesline, and throw your T-shirts, socks, underwear, sheets, towels, and kids' clothes into the dryer.
- ☺ Drying textiles on drying racks and clotheslines will

make them last much longer, save you money, and treat the Earth more kindly.

☺ When you use your dryer, add wool balls to make your clothes dry faster, bumpy dryer balls to make your towels fluffier, and an aluminum ball to eliminate all static.

☺ Never use fabric softener or dryer sheets—period.

Now, what are you waiting for? It's time to dry your textiles!

5

Time to Pump Some Iron
(or Blow Off Some Steam)

I find it soothing to take something wrinkled and
make it smooth. It feels anticipatory.
—ALEXANDRA STODDARD,
INTERIOR DESIGNER AND AUTHOR

Ever come across a word that looks odd to you? Like the letters
have landed in the wrong order on the page? And the longer you
stare at that word, the more bizarre it appears. *Is that really how
it's spelled? Is that even a word?*

Not long ago for me, that word was *wrinkly*.

My questioning sent me to the dictionary, where I came across an even crazier-looking word: *gewrinclod*, an Old English term meaning sinuous, and the origin word for wrinkly, wrinkles, and all such related expressions.

I wouldn't have been surprised if I'd discovered a word of Chinese origin instead. After all, ironing was invented in China. More than a thousand years ago, they'd heap hot coals into small metal bowls and then move them, via long handles, over stretched textiles to smooth out the wrinkles. Obviously, the Chinese were fine dressers even back then—wearing gorgeously embroidered and flowing gowns. No wonder thousands of young people in China today are part of the Hanfu movement, wearing clothing inspired by their ancient dynasties.

But ironing with hot bowls was just the beginning. Over centuries, ironing was performed around the world with a wide variety of tools—among them, flat round stones, glass smoothers that looked like giant upside-down mushrooms, screw presses used to flatten large damp linens, and mangles.

Ah, the mangle. As a small boy, I thought the mangle was the fanciest of all household appliances. That's because my neighbor, Ruby, a woman who'd traveled around the world *four times*, owned one. She was super chic, with friends in London and a personal shopper in Pennsylvania. I loved her travel stories and her big-city ways. Ruby would often invite me over for dinner, and we'd dine on filet mignon, mashed potatoes, green beans, and rolls—every dinner was identical and wonderful.

But it was her mangle, "the ironer," that most captured my attention. This machine, invented during the 1500s, uses rollers to press clothes. Much later, during the nineteenth century, "mangle women" would hand-crank fabric through steam- and later gas-heated rollers, taking it from wrinkled on one side of the machine to smooth on the other. Ruby's mangle was electric, and because she owned one, I aspired to have one, too. I assumed that once I had my own mangle, I would be cosmopolitan—just like her.

I'm sad to say I still don't have a mangle. I just don't have room to fit one more thing in my combination laundry room–master bathroom. *Someday*. In the meantime, I have a steam-generating iron that I adore—more on that later.

The Vinyasa of Ironing

In today's society, ironing often seems like a chore of yesteryear. But it wasn't that long ago that ironing was something practically everyone did. As a kid, my mom pressed most of our clothes. For me, she ironed my shirts but not my jeans—even today I like wearing rumpled jeans. So I remember being surprised one day to find her ironing my brother Jarrod's jeans. She explained that his shirts didn't need ironing, "So ironing his jeans shows I care." Taking care of family members' clothes was a big way we showed love in my family.

As I grew older, I started ironing my own clothes because I wanted to learn how. Eventually, I took over all the ironing; I had the luxury of time, unlike my working mother, and I enjoyed making our clothes look splendid—crisp button-downs, pants ironed with sharp creases, and impeccable handkerchiefs ironed into four stacked squares—ironed flat, folded and ironed, and then folded and ironed again.

Suffice it to say, I love ironing. There's a gracefulness and a meditative feel to the task. Plus a pure satisfaction as you smooth out the wrinkles, making a shirt or pair of pants look just so. When the world feels out of whack and the bad news keeps coming, it's a relief to perform a household routine that gives both pleasure and a bit of control.

I'm not alone in this feeling. Of all household activities, ironing may be the most frequent topic addressed by poets. In "Ode to Ironing," Pablo Neruda suggests a higher purpose with this line: "the hands keep moving, the sacred surfaces get smoothed." I know of several other ironing-themed poems—including "Ironing" by Vicki Feaver and "Ironing After Midnight" by Marsha Truman Cooper. But my favorite may be Julia Alvarez's "Ironing Their Clothes," in which this Dominican American poet writes of expressing love for her family through attentive ironing, shrugging the world off her father's shoulders by pressing his shirts, caressing the "collars, scallops, ties, pleats" of her mother's blouses, and tickling the "underarms of my big sister's petticoat."

Do you regularly iron your clothes? Or perhaps you prefer to steam them? If you don't iron or steam your clothes, I'm here to suggest you do—some of them anyway, at least some of the time.

I understand that ironing may feel unnecessary. After all, lots of our clothes are made with modern fabrics that don't tend to wrinkle—at least not that much. Plus, the idea of adding ironing or steaming to a long list of other household chores and life to-dos may seem unfathomable. And perhaps ironing feels like a hassle: Maybe, like me, you have to move items around to create a space for ironing and set up your ironing board—or you may have to collect all the stuff that you've heaped onto your ironing board and move it elsewhere in order to actually iron.

Despite all that, both ironing and/or steaming are necessary—sometimes. Here are four important points to encourage you in your ironing.

First, you have more time than you think. Now that you'll be washing everything on express, your laundry routine will be much shorter. Plus, you'll no longer be using dry cleaning, so you'll be saving all that time that you used to spend on gathering up your dry-clean-only items, driving to the dry cleaner, waiting in line, picking it up again, etc.

To make the most of your available time, I recommend multitasking—something you're no doubt familiar with. When I'm doing the laundry, I usually multitask, ironing clean yet wrinkled clothes that have accumulated—typically while a first load is drying and a second load is in the wash. After all, I need to stay close to my laundry room anyway. Watching an episode or two of my favorite TV show or listening to podcasts while I iron is another great way I pass the time.

Second, understand which fabrics actually need ironing. While some items require pressing, such as an oxford cotton shirt, others don't. Take it from me: Steaming linen can give it polish, but you never *need* to iron a linen shirt, suit, or skirt. Wrinkly (there's that word again) is kind of the look of this lightweight, summery fabric. The same goes for seersucker. I also don't iron flannel shirts. While doing so can dress them up, ironing decreases the loft of the flannel and lessens the shirts' warmth.

But some garments simply demand ironing. For example, I iron all my cotton shirts (excluding T-shirts) and all my dress pants. In many situations, a crisply ironed outfit provides a confident, pulled-together look.

Third, ironing helps prevents stains. Ironing smooths the rough fibers of a garment, making it less likely to trap a stain. In addition, if you use spray starch during ironing, you're more likely to get rid of stains that occur later. (More on this ahead.)

Fourth, and most important, an iron or a steamer is the tool you can use to get the look you want. That's true for your everyday appearance, your weekend style, or a special occasion. That's also the case for your kid's upcoming job or college interview, or your partner's big presentation.

If you're on the fence about ironing, try this: Iron two of your shirts or blouses. For one, simply use the steam setting of your iron, or use a steamer to relax the wrinkles. For the second, go all out: Iron with steam and starch, adding creases where they're supposed to be, and cleaning up the look of the pockets and the seams (see all my how-tos, beginning on page 70).

Now, put on the steamed shirt and check yourself out in a mirror, thinking about how this shirt's appearance serves, or doesn't serve, various purposes in your life. Then, do the same with the ironed shirt. Finally, repeat this process once more with a third, unironed shirt or blouse.

Which do you like best for work, for play, for a special event? Your answers will vary based on your life. Maybe you work in the back of the house at a restaurant and typically wear a uniform, but you like to get decked out for clubbing. Or perhaps you work at a financial institution that requires a suit, but you love to relax your look on weekends. Or maybe you throw on jeans and a sweatshirt for your college classes most days, but an upcoming wedding means you want to step up your style. Obviously, understanding how to best care for your clothes, and how each item looks and feels when steamed or pressed, will let you know what you prefer for each occasion.

You may decide that steaming is what you want to do for your work clothes, but that a friend's engagement party or a class reunion requires more attention spent at your ironing board. Or perhaps you'll find that full-blown ironing not only gives you the look you want most days but is conducive to your peace of mind—a little like yoga. Then, by all means, iron away.

Steamer or Iron?

Whatever look you desire, I've included lots of helpful information regarding ironing and steaming in the following pages. To decide which you prefer, ironing or steaming, let's take a closer look:

To begin, know that you can steam everything. Steaming is best for providing a soft, wrinkle-free finish for silky blouses and skirts, drapes, and any garments for which you like a softer finish. For example, I like my oxford cloth shirts to look soft, not crisp. In addition, while a steamer can't clean, it does revitalize garments between washes and can be used to remove odors from your clothes, plus your sofa and drapes (without taking them down). Be sure to read your product's manufacturer guide for all the directions and how-tos.

Ironing, on the other hand, is best for creating a hard finish. Think crisply pressed shirts, fine pant creases, perfectly ironed napkins.

Of course, the perfect choice is a steam-generating iron, which combines the best attributes of both the steamer and the iron, delivering killer results for both purposes—the steamed soft look and the crisp hard finish. I've owned my steam-generating iron for nine years and I love it for myriad reasons. For starters, it's a two-in-one appliance—a steamer and an iron. That means, unlike other irons, it can be used both horizontally and vertically. Second, unlike most steamers, a steam-generating iron uses pressurized steam, which is way more effective for both steaming and ironing. And third, you'll likely never need to replace it. These high-quality appliances can be serviced professionally or, with a little troubleshooting over the phone with the manufacturer, you can fix it yourself with a replacement part.

There's a financial aspect to these small electric appliances, however. You can buy a good-quality iron for roughly $25. You can buy a good-quality steamer for approximately $60. And you can buy both and still not approach the cost of that steam-generating iron, which can run you $200 or more. That said, if you live in a small apartment and don't have a lot of storage, I'd recommend investing in a steam-generating iron. Besides, if you don't dry clean anymore, you've paid for that appliance in no time.

The How-Tos of Steaming

If you like the idea of using a steamer best, buy the most expensive steamer you can afford. Most inexpensive handheld steamers provide less-than-robust steam and must be refilled with water every fifteen minutes or so; that means every time you add more water, you must wait for the water to heat and your steaming will take that much longer to complete. Alternatively, most large steamers boast more wattage and water capacity, heat up in under a minute, offer adjustable controls, and provide continuous steam for up to an hour.

When steaming clothes, hang your garments first; then touch only the top edge of the steamer head to the garment, keep the steamer hose straight, and move the steamer head slowly up and down each garment so as not to accidentally burn yourself. As you steam, pull the fabric gently (not tautly) with your other hand; this helps remove the wrinkles and makes the process go faster. And whenever possible, place the steamer inside the garment (don't turn it inside out) and steam to the front (away from you). This way, you can see what you're doing as the wrinkles disappear from the garment. Steaming from the inside means you're also less likely to make an error—if you create a water spot, it will happen inside the garment.

While many people steam in their laundry rooms or bathrooms, you can steam anywhere. Also, if you're going to steam a lot, install a hook high on the wall so it's easier to steam—doing so means that you won't be crouching on the floor to steam a hem. Finally, when you're done steaming a garment, let it dry for a minute or two before you return the clothing item to your closet—you don't want it to wrinkle again while it's damp.

To Sum Up

Use a steamer:

- To get rid of wrinkles, steaming from the inside of the garment.
- To touch up your favorite shirt, skirt, or pants in a flash.
- To bring a cardigan back to life without washing.
- To freshen up window treatments without having to take them down.

Use an iron:

- To create creases right where you want them.
- To give your clothing a crisp, polished look.

Use a steam-generating iron to do all of the above, plus:

- To press even hard-to-iron fabrics like heavy cotton and twill.

Now you're ready to begin ironing and steaming! Specific instructions follow on ironing shirts and pants, but please note that these instructions assume your clothing has no stains. If it does, remove the stains first to avoid setting them with the iron. More on that can be found in chapter 7.

How to Iron a Shirt

To start, gather your ironing supplies: an iron (a steam-generating iron is preferred), distilled or soft water (whichever your iron requires), a bottle of water for misting, and spray starch. Some irons specify soft water from the tap, because the extra minerals enable the water to get hotter. If you have hard water, you'll shorten the life of the iron.

For best results, iron your shirt not long after you've removed it from the dryer when it's still damp. If it's dry, mist the shirt generously with water right before beginning the ironing process. And always move the iron in the direction of its point. Once you've ironed a shirt or two, you'll fall into a rhythm, much like doing sun salutations—only you'll have a rack full of clean shirts at the end.

Once you're ready to begin, follow these steps:

- First, make sure your sole plate (the bottom of the iron) is clean, fill your iron with the required water for steam, select the setting based on your shirt's fabric, and turn on your iron.
- While the iron heats, spray your entire (damp) shirt with starch; you can keep the shirt on its hanger for this step. Give the shirt a minute to dry, letting the starch set into the fabric, so you won't create any white "snow" (dried starch) while ironing.
- Start with the collar, first re-moving any collar stays (if applicable). Iron the under-side of the collar, moving in  the direction of its point from one end to the middle

and then from the other end to the middle. Then flip the collar over and repeat this process. Do not refold the collar and iron the crease. If your shirt has a yoke (a separate section across the shoulders), iron the yoke flat, working from each side to the center.

☺ Next, iron the cuffs and the sleeves. Unbutton one cuff and iron its inside and then its outside, carefully mov-ing the iron's point around the buttons. If it's a French cuff, unfold the cuff and iron it flat; don't refold and iron the crease. Next, ensure that the two layers of the sleeve's fabric align; even refold, if possible, along the previously ironed crease. Then iron the sleeve from its top edge to its bottom edge; flip the sleeve over to iron from its top edge to its bottom edge again on the other side. Repeat this entire process with the other cuff and sleeve. Alternatively, with a steam-generating iron (which you can use vertically), you can iron sleeves to perfection while the shirt is on a hanger. Roll up a thick magazine (I use *Vogue*) and place it into one of the sleeves. Then iron the sleeve, actually pressing the iron to the cloth, all the way around its circumference. (Again, be careful so you don't burn yourself.)

☺ Next, iron half of the shirt's front. Place the side of the shirt with the buttons at the wide end of the ironing board, hugging the inside of the shirt's shoulder around the board's corner. Iron the shirt near the buttons, carefully moving the iron's point around them. Then press the iron from the shoulder down to the hem. Ensure the top of the shirt looks especially smooth since that area will get more attention when you wear it.

- Then pull the shirt around the ironing board to iron half of the back of the shirt, moving the iron down the shirt, from shoulder to hem. Pull the shirt further around the ironing board to iron the other side of the back of the shirt. If the shirt has a centered back pleat, pull the pleat up with your fingers and reset the pleat by ironing flat.

- Complete the circle by pulling the other half of the shirt's front to the top of the board and iron this last section, paying close  attention to the placket (the length along the shirt with the buttonholes). If your shirt has one or two pockets, iron each from the bottom up, pulling each taut as you do.

- Finally, like letting a manicure set or meat rest before carving, allow the garment to dry for a minute or two before hanging. This ensures the creases remain and no new wrinkles appear in your freshly ironed shirt.

How to Iron Pants

Same as with shirts, begin by gathering your ironing supplies: an iron (a steam-generating iron is preferred), distilled or soft water (whichever your iron requires), a bottle of water for misting, a small bucket of water, and a pressing cloth.

You can buy a pressing cloth designed especially for ironing, you can make one by cutting a roughly twelve-inch by thirty-inch square of fabric from an old sheet, or you can use a handkerchief—it's smaller, but in a pinch, it's effective. When pressing blouses, delicate items, or garments with a water-repellant finish, lay the cloth atop your garment as you iron; this prevents the iron from causing a sheen, a scorch, water spots, and pressing marks on your items. It also safeguards the iron from a print transferring on to your iron or a cheap fabric from melting on to your iron.

If you typically wear casual pants, there's likely no reason to iron them. I never iron my jeans or my khakis. If, however, you wear casual pants as part of a company uniform, say waiting tables, you may want to consider ironing them. For dress pants, however, it's always a good idea to iron them after washing them—which should just be once or twice a season. (Remember: Ironing a pair of pants takes far less time than taking your pants to the dry cleaner and retrieving them later.)

When ironing pants, you'll always want to use a pressing cloth to avoid creating shiny spots on the fabric. I learned the method I share below from an Eastern European tailor at Embry's department store, where I worked as a sales consultant ages ago. The tailor generously taught me lots of ironing tricks, including how to use a pressing cloth for crisp sharp creases. And because I often ironed garments for my customers, rather than bringing their special requests to her, she also generously alerted me when she'd brought fresh, hot doughnuts to share.

Before ironing, make sure your pants are still a bit damp right out of the dryer or mist them generously with water. And again, always move the iron in the direction of its point.

- First, make sure your sole plate (the bottom of the iron) is clean, fill your iron with the required water, select the setting with the lowest heat required by the pant fabric, and turn on your iron.
- Pull out the pocket liners and iron them; doing so will ensure they lie flat under the pressed pant legs.
- Next, leaving the pocket liners pulled out of the pants, iron the waistband and the top of the pants. Press and lift the iron as you move around the top of the pants.
- Then, if you're ironing casual pants, simply tuck the liners back into the pockets and iron each pant leg flat, with no middle-of-the-leg creases. Two ironed pant legs equals done and done.
- If, however, you're ironing dress pants, you'll want to add a front crease and a back crease to the middle of each pant leg. To do so, tuck the liners back into the pockets and then hang the waistband off the end of the ironing board. Next, stretch out both pant legs along the ironing board, stacking one on top of the other on their sides. From the cuffs, align the seams and the front and back creases should fall into place,  running along the edges of the pant legs. Briefly run the iron over the stacked pant legs. Next, fold the top leg back, toward the waistband.
- Dip a pressing cloth into a small bucket of water, wring it out, and lay it flat across the lower pant leg. Pressing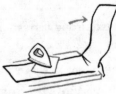

and lifting, move the iron along the pant leg atop the pressing cloth. Then remove the pressing cloth, unfold the top leg back over the lower pant leg, and place the pressing cloth across the once-again stacked pant legs. Again, press and lift the iron along the pant legs.

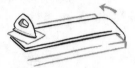

⊕ Next, remove the pressing cloth and flip over the pants to repeat these steps on the other side. Begin by wetting and wringing out the pressing cloth again.

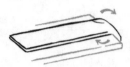

⊕ Once you've pressed the legs on the other side, remove the pressing cloth for the final time, and touch up any missed areas.

⊕ Take a last look at the pants, touch up any missed wrinkles, and let them dry on the ironing board for a minute or two before hanging.

Shirts and pants are the most complicated items you can iron. If you can iron these, you can iron anything. Be sure to give yourself some time—like anything worth doing, ironing takes a bit of practice. Just keep in mind a couple rules of thumb: Always iron a garment top to bottom and front to back. And once you've finished, be sure to hang up the garment on the correct hanger so that it hangs flat.

Speaking of hangers, it's our next topic—clothing storage, including hanging, folding, and a bunch of surprising tips and insights that come along with it. Let's get started.

6

The Comprehensive Closet

You've got to know when to hold 'em, know when to
fold 'em.

Not long ago I was talking to a reporter about how I became
an expert on textiles and their care. While I majored in the subject in college and have decades of experience, I really think it's
my lifelong passion for and curiosity about textiles and their
care that has led to my command of the subjects. (It's not every boy who requests the men's fashion bible *Dress for Success*

for his eleventh birthday.) These topics never grow tired for me, whether it's about a garment's inception, design, and creation, or its eventual place in our lives and in our closets.

Long ago people owned so few clothes that they had no need for closets. Instead, at workday's end, they'd just hang their smattering of garments on wall pegs. In fact, clothes hangers weren't even invented until the mid 1800s. Now we consider hangers indispensible.

Back in the seventeenth century and before, only wealthy people had a sufficient number of clothes to require storage—and these extra garments would be placed in armoires and wardrobes. In fact, closets weren't for clothes storage at all, but instead were private, even secret spaces reserved for leisure time, including spiritual contemplation and art appreciation. For example, in the Bible, believers are advised to pray in their closets. And people today still talk about coming out of the closet when publically revealing a secret.

There's at least one historic exception to a closet's use for actual clothes storage: King Louis XVI added a Clothes Cabinet (with two capital Cs) to his private apartment in Versailles in 1778. Boasting two large windows, white-and-gold arabesque wood paneling, a gilded mirror, and a fireplace, this space (reached via a secret door in the king's bedchamber) was used not only to store his wardrobe (hidden behind elaborately carved doors) but also to consider his country's challenges—and perhaps to plot his escape during the French Revolution.

I imagine it was like one of those fancy walk-in closets of today, where you can not only select your daily attire but surf the web or read a good book while lying on a chaise lounge, glass of wine and pashmina throw at the ready. Given my own distinct lack of walk-in closets, I can only assume this is standard walk-in closet behavior—or at least it would be for me.

The Dakota, the famous New York City apartment building—completed in 1884 and home, over the years, to numerous celebrities, including Leonard Bernstein, Roberta Flack, and John Lennon—was the first luxury American multifamily residence to introduce walk-in closets, reportedly with locking doors, built-in shoe shelves, marble basins, and electrical outlets.

A few decades later, around the turn of the twentieth century, closets morphed into clothing-storage spaces for the rest of us—although most of them were narrow and simple "reach-in" closets.

As a kid, I remember Granny Dude calling any closet in her house "the press"—as in, "Patric, will you put this in the press?" Only she pronounced it "pray-us" in her Southern way. An old term of Irish origin, using the word "*press*" for the closet seems to have been popular in the South, particularly in Virginia, Ohio, and Kentucky.

Walk-in closets wouldn't really grow in popularity until much later. Given more space in my home, I'd happily convert my bedroom into a walk-in closet—complete with a fireplace à la King Louis.

It's Not Rocket Science

Today, clothing storage has reached a fever pitch, with rules and regulations about folding, hanging, and storing. My take on all this? If it works for you, it's the right method. But, for heaven's sake, please fold and hang your clothes as soon as they're done drying. Your clean clothes heaped into baskets are just getting more wrinkled by the minute.

I've always enjoyed folding. When I was in college, I began working for McAlpin's department store. When business was slow, we could always stay busy folding clothes. I remember my first Christmas there. It was so busy that we'd start on one end of the clothing tables, folding sweaters, and by the time we got to the other end, we had to start folding all over again.

Of course, there are lots of ways to fold things. I remember discovering a new way to fold towels at my neighbor Ruby's house. I liked her way so much better than my mom's method that I still fold all of my towels her way to this day (for more on Ruby's method, see page 87).

While we don't need to take these activities too seriously—most are common sense—there are some basic guidelines that can help us prolong the lifespan of our clothes, keep our clothes (nearly) wrinkle free, and make us look a whole lot better. Consider how you feel when you throw on a T-shirt and crumpled jeans, retrieved from your bedroom floor, compared to your attitude when you select a cleaned and pressed outfit from your closet.

I've been working in retail so long that folding and hanging clothes is like brushing my teeth or even, dare I say, breathing. I don't have to think about how to fold practically anything anymore. If you've worked at a clothing store, you know exactly what I mean. Folding shirts and jeans to the exact same size is so second nature that I could perform it as a party trick—while blindfolded. The benefit? Folding all of your matching items, say T-shirts, to the same size allows everything to fit nicely in your drawers. That means you can see everything you own, easily

select what you'd like to wear on any given day, and perhaps even
resist the urge to buy more.

I invite you to take your own clothing storage inspiration
from retail. The next time you're shopping, check out the clothing displays at your favorite shop. Which clothing items are fea-
tured together? Which garments are hung on hangers, and which
are folded and neatly stacked on tables? Often all the dress shirts
are hung up to prevent wrinkling, while sweaters are folded to
prevent stretching. Similarly, dress pants are likely hung on dedicated pants hangers, while jeans are folded and stacked. And
how is each category (for example, jeans or sweaters) folded—in
halves, rolled up, or with fronts showing? Which do you prefer?

Now consider the store's arrangements of accessories. Are
interesting containers—clear plastic racks, woven baskets, wine
racks—used to store scarves or belts? And what do you already
own that could cleverly serve this purpose? How do they display
a complete outfit—on a dress form, a mannequin, or perhaps
an antique brass or wooden hanger? Could the addition of an
artistic hanger or a singular wall peg near your closet help calm
your busy morning—by enabling you to display every item, from
head to toe, that you plan to wear?

Usually, a great deal of thought is put into retail clothing
displays, making them attractive and engaging to browse. Doing
the same in your own bedroom can make "shopping" your closet
that much more fun.

A friend's teenage son recently learned that after a bedroom makeover—one he not only hadn't asked for but didn't
want. He was accustomed to his space and liked it the way it
was—even though he'd outgrown the furniture, piles of clean
and dirty clothes littered much of his floor space, and the walls

hadn't been painted since his birth. Despite his reluctance, his parents were convinced he'd welcome the changes if he had a say in the process—including the selection of paint, a new IKEA bed (which he built himself), and lots of storage. Suddenly, his clothes were folded and placed, like with like, in his dresser; his socks, underwear, and bedding found accessible homes in drawers built right into his bed; and all his oxford and flannel shirts were hanging neatly in his closet. He had to admit—the changes were pretty awesome. Who knew that getting dressed could be so easy and enjoyable?

Folding vs. Hanging

So how do you decide whether to hang or fold an item of clothing? Garments to hang include dress shirts, blouses, dresses, skirts, dress pants, jackets, and suits. Clothing items to fold include sweaters, T-shirts, jeans, lingerie, underwear, and socks. From there, I've got many more suggestions. Let's start with the clothes you hang.

For All Your Hang-Ups

First, for maximum storage in your closet, use matching hangers, as they're meant to fit together nicely. (More on this in the sidebar below.) That means the shape, the color, everything matching. You don't need a variety of hangers distracting you from the closet's real stars: your clothes. While I love heavy wooden hangers, my narrow closet requires slim, velvet-covered hangers for maximum space efficiency. The velvet also offers staying power—I know that I'll never find a shirt that has slid to the floor.

Second, hang all of your clothes facing the same way, and keep like items together by category: for example, sleeveless tops, short-sleeved shirts, long-sleeved shirts, or blazers. You can even create subcategories, say, patterned long-sleeved shirts and plain long-sleeved shirts. Again, garments that should be hung typically include your fancier clothes—dress shirts, blouses, dresses, skirts, dress pants, jackets, and suits. While this is common sense, the more organization you bring to your closet, the more enjoyable getting dressed is—whether for an ordinary Monday, your child's eighth-grade graduation, or an epic concert.

· ·

Selecting the Best Hangers

I'm not the first person to say this, but don't use wire hangers. They're not strong enough to support your clothes, they can damage your garments, and there are many better options. Try any of the following instead:

☺ Tubular plastic hangers come at a great price, often ten for a dollar at a discount store. While they aren't strong, I don't hate them. They never rust, there's no color transfer from the hangers onto your clothes, and your clothes will hang just fine. Their only negative is that they don't come in men's- and women's-size hangers—which simply refers to two widths. Tubular plastic hangers do come in children's sizes, however; if you've got kids' clothes, children-size hangers serve these clothes best.

- Flat plastic hangers, like the ones often used at retail stores, come in endless sizes and colors. Stronger than tubular plastic hangers, these still tend to be inexpensive—and, fun tip, if you order directly from a retail supply store, you can replace all the hangers in your closets at once.

- Velvet-covered hangers are a great option if your closet space is lacking. Not only can you pack more clothes into a closet when they're hung on these thin hangers, your clothes will never slip off—and, if you use the original brand, they guarantee not to release velvet onto your clothes, even if you hang up wet items. Finally, velvet-covered hangers prevent your clothes from stretching.

- Wooden hangers come in many options, i.e., curved for suit jackets and blazers, flat for blouses and shirts, clipped for skirts and pants, and many others. They look luxurious in your closet and their heft makes them strong. The downside is their size—they take up a lot of space. If you do use wooden hangers, be sure to keep a set of tubular or plastic hangers in your laundry room for hanging up wet clothes. If you hang wet clothes on wooden hangers, there's a chance wood stain will transfer onto your garments.

- I also love wooden hangers because they remind me of Louise, my bonus grandmother. She sewed clothes, knitted, crocheted, embroidered, did needlepoint, and more. In fact, I love doing needlepoint today because of her. Louise used to crochet covers for wooden hangers. Even after she became blind in her late eighties, she continued to crochet hangers, simply counting her stitches to ensure each fit perfectly. Still hanging in my closet is an orange one (my favorite color) that she made especially for me.

☺ Finally, if you prefer flat plastic or wooden hangers, consider the various size options. Both of these hanger types come in men's- and women's-size hangers—their size is determined simply by the typical width of men's and women's shoulders. However, if you're a narrow-shouldered gentleman, you may prefer women's hangers, and if you're a broad-shouldered woman, you may want to invest in men's hangers. And if you're petite, you may find that children's hangers best fit your clothing.

. . . .

Return to the Fold

Now let's turn our attention to folding. The 1914 textbook *Laundering* includes step-by-step drawings for folding common garments of the time, including corset covers, chemises, night-dresses, and drawers (that is, underwear). Despite our more modern attire, the guidelines for folding haven't really changed—the goal is to fold similar items in the same way for maximum efficiency and best display in your dresser.

To fold a shirt, I begin with the garment spread out on my bed or a table with its back facing up. I fold in each side to meet in the middle and then fold the sleeves down toward the hem of the shirt—the shirt should now look like a neat rectangle; I then bring the bottom hem to the top, and then flip the shirt over. Voilà! For a T-shirt, once I fold in the sides and sleeves, I fold it in thirds. For both types of shirts, I tuck them in a drawer, one shirt after the other, vertically—like I'm filing a folder so I can see them all at once.

To fold a sweater, again I begin with it spread out on my bed or a table with its back facing up. I fold in the sides and then the sleeves to create a neat rectangle; I then fold the sweater in thirds and flip it over. I line up sweaters horizontally in a bureau drawer to display all of my options. If you don't have room in your dresser to store all of your sweaters, fold each sweater in thirds and hang each over the bottom rung of a hanger in your closet. Please don't hang knitted items like shirts or sweaters on hangers, such that the hanger corners fill out the shoulders—hung this way, they'll stretch and lose their shape.

To fold casual pants, place one leg atop the other, fold in half, and then fold in thirds before lining them up in a drawer. If you don't have room to store casual pants in your dresser, simply hang these as you do your dress pants: folded in half and crimped at the cuffs and waistband on dedicated pants hangers, or folded in half and then draped over the lowest rung of a regular hanger.

To fold socks, I lay one atop the other and roll them up, or fold them in halves or thirds for long socks. I store all my socks in vertical stacks in one drawer.

For bedding, ensure that it is completely dry before folding. To fold a flat sheet, fold it in half the long way; you may want to do this on the floor so you can smooth out any wrinkles. Then fold it in half the long way again; now you've got a very long, skinny rectangle. Next, fold in half once in the other direction, and then again (and maybe again) until it's the size of a pillowcase. Done!

For a fitted sheet, turn it inside out and place each of your hands inside one corner of one short end of the sheet—the elastic side is facing you; bring your hands (and the corners) together and fold one corner over the other corner. Keep these corners on one hand while, with your other hand, you grab a third corner and fold it over the top two corners; do the same with the final corner. That's the hard part. Next, fold the sheet in half and then again (and maybe again) until it's the size of a pillowcase. Done again!

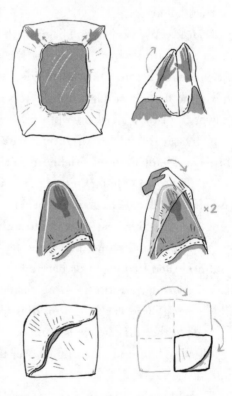

To fold a pillowcase, simply fold it three times, beginning by folding it in half the short way. Once everything is folded, place all pieces of each set—flat sheet, fitted sheet, and pillowcase—

into the second pillowcase. If it's a twin set, simply place the top and bottom sheets into the pillowcase.

. . . .

Ruby's Towel-Folding Method

My neighbor Ruby's approach to folding towels is a particularly good solution if you have open shelves or place your towels on display. To begin, fold the towel in thirds the long way. Then fold the two ends toward each other where they meet in the middle. Finally, fold the towel in half. Ta-da—the edges are hidden inside.

In my bathroom, I have a train rack (reminiscent of the luggage racks on passenger trains of yesteryear) on which I display our bath towels and use a slightly different take on Ruby's method: Again, fold the towel in thirds the long way. Then fold the two ends toward each other where they meet in middle. Finally, roll up the towel. This roll-up version also looks great when displaying towels in a wine rack repurposed for the bathroom.

. . . .

Dealing with Seasonal Storage

I remember one lovely April as a kid when all of a sudden our area was socked with a freak snowstorm. Mom had already washed and stored our winter gear, including all of our coats, at the back of a very long storage closet in our basement. On a busy school morning, there was no time to crawl to the back of that closet to retrieve them. I remember Mom telling us to put on our nylon windbreakers while she warmed up the car, and then urging us to make a run for the car through the snow flurries.

While few of us completely turn over our wardrobes from one season to the next, many of us likely store wool sweaters in the summer and swimsuit cover-ups and the like in the winter. Perhaps you're one of those folks who regularly send everything to the dry cleaner at the end of the season and then store the items in dry-cleaning bags. Well, you're done with that routine— now you'll be washing those items yourself, quickly and easily. But once that's done, what's the best way to store these clean, out-of-season garments?

If you're lucky enough to have storage space, I recommend draping an old clean sheet (simply snip a hole in its middle for the hooks of your hangers to fit through) over these clothes to keep the dust off. Using a sheet, rather than plastic bags or even suit bags, lets the clothes breathe. (Plus, you're being kinder to the Earth by not using plastic.)

Be sure, too, to include a small block or ball of cedar in each pocket, or place a hanging cedar block (attached to a hook) every foot or so in this storage area. Cedar zaps moisture from the air to prevent mildew, protects garments from fabric-eating moths and other pests, and lends a fresh scent to your clothes. (Once a year, lightly rub cedar blocks with sandpaper to revive the cedar's natural scent.)

For seasonal items for which you don't have closet space, consider using space-saving vacuum storage bags—the bags you suck all the air out of with your vacuum. Before using these bags, I wash everything first and then stuff my clothes in—there's no need to iron, obviously, as the clothes will become very wrinkly. When I take these clothes out at the start of a new season, I simply wash them again. Especially for people with limited storage space, these bags are a great solution and easily slide under most beds, completely out of sight.

Let's review:

- There are lots of ways to store clothing—use the methods that work best for you. That said, I recommend hanging suit jackets and blazers, dress shirts and pants, and skirts and dresses on hangers. For T-shirts, sweaters, casual pants like jeans and leggings, and socks and underwear, fold and tuck into dresser drawers.
- Most important, hang or fold your clothes right after they're done drying.
- Let retail storage systems inspire you to make "shopping" your own closet more fun, with creative displays and a place to show off tomorrow's outfit.
- For maximum efficiency in your closet, use matching hangers that all face the same direction, and hang similar items together.
- For maximum efficiency in your dresser, fold like items to the same size, using identical folding methods; then store them vertically so you can see everything that's available in each drawer.
- For seasonal items, place a sheet over hanging items and/or use space-saving vacuum storage bags and then tuck them out of sight.

7

Time for Your Disappearing Act

"Out, damn'd spot! Out, I say!"
—WILLIAM SHAKESPEARE

It's a flat-out cliché to use this Lady Macbeth quote to refer to stain removal. Hundreds—literally hundreds—of stain-removal articles, both online and in print, use that passage. I even found a 1916 *Good Housekeeping* feature, "Home Remedies for Spots," that mentions it: "The time-honored Macbethian incantation, 'Out, damned spot,' pales into insignificance beside the efficacy of a slip of a maid with a puff of absorbent cotton and a zeal worthy the cause." But I'm guessing few families back then had maids to perform their dirty work—with zeal no less.

The popularity of the quotation makes sense: After all, this conniving Shakespearean character is talking about removing actual bloodstains after she and her husband have murdered a king. Much more recently, comedian Jerry Seinfeld joked about a similar subject, noting that if you're trying to remove blood from fabric, "maybe laundry isn't your biggest problem."

In this chapter, I'll share the three basic types of stains and the easy solutions I recommend to eliminate them. I'll also include Laundry Campers' most requested stain tricks—those for lipstick, red wine, barbecue sauce, and perspiration. Plus, I'll offer dozens more solutions in my comprehensive stain guide at the end of the chapter.

Stain Stories from the Trenches

Whenever I'm leading a Laundry Camp, I always save the topic of stains for the end. Stains are my fireworks, and they're the main reason many attendees sign up for camp in the first place. Why? Because stains so often aggravate and confound us.

I always invite participants to bring stained garments to camp. Usually just one or two take me up on the offer, but, wow, are they glad they did. While the whole class watches and learns, I remove the stains, right on the spot (see what I did there?).

Sometimes campers are so enthusiastic about my success with laundry that they propose, only half jokingly, that they hire me to do their wash. *Um, I don't think so*. I happily do my laundry and my loved ones' laundry—but that's where I draw the line. However, I'm delighted to teach *you* how to do your wash better. That's the whole idea behind Laundry Camps.

When it comes to stains, I'm glad to be Johnny-on-the-spot, quite literally. Once, one of my longtime customers, Ronnie, called me nearly in tears. Her grandson was about to have his bar mitzvah and her husband, due to serious health issues, couldn't attend the ceremony, which was being held in another city. So, to share a bit of himself, he was lending his *tallit* to his grandson. This blue-and-white prayer shawl was purchased by his parents in Israel in 1948 (the very year of the country's founding) for his own bar mitzvah.

It was a beautiful gesture. Unfortunately, to prepare for the big day, my customer had handwashed the tallit with a so-called delicate detergent. Disaster! The blue had run all over the white. Now what—could I salvage this heirloom?

Anyone who knows me understands that I'm a sucker for a grandmother-grandson story. After all, I had two amazing grannies. How could I possibly refuse her request?

So the next day, Ronnie dropped off the tallit, carefully tucked inside a bag, for me to attempt a laundry miracle. When I pulled it out, I saw she was exactly right: the shawl looked completely ruined.

In the meantime, I'd done a little research. It turned out that the white of the tallit is more important than the blue. So the job wasn't so much about bringing the blue back as it was removing it from the white.

I got to work. First, I spread out the shawl atop a bath towel on my kitchen island. Next, using Q-tips dipped in oxalic acid, I began carefully dabbing at each jot of blue, wherever it didn't belong. The work was painstaking—removing blue dot after blue dot. Finally, it was time for the last steps: Holding my breath, I held the tallit under the faucet, rinsing away any vestiges of errant blue in my kitchen sink, and then laid the garment back atop my table to dry. Not long after, I had the great pleasure of doing a big reveal and got to see Ronnie's sheer delight when I unveiled the brand-new-looking tallit.

I've got a million stain-related stories, but another that springs to mind involves a wedding: I was working at my boutique on a Saturday morning when I got a call from a frantic bridesmaid. The bride had just been zipped up in her wedding dress when an affectionate toddler had run pell-mell to hug her—while carrying a permanent marker. Now black lines wriggled up the right side of her gown. Heavens! The bridal party had found one of my stain-removal videos on YouTube, but the rubbing alcohol wasn't working. What else would I recommend? Better yet, would I drive to the church, just five miles away, to remove the stain in person?

Of course! I'm always game for stain-removal thrills. But there was a problem: I couldn't leave my store unattended. While I tracked down a willing employee, one of the bridesmaids even considered covering for me. Eventually, one of my generous staff members came in early, and I practically ran past her out the door, carrying all my stain-removal gear.

When I arrived at the church, the bridesmaids rushed me like a first responder to the anxious bride and her besmirched gown. *Some way or another, we're going to make your dress look perfect,* I assured her. I felt certain that I could remove the stain, but—worst-case scenario—I knew a quick stitch could hide the pen marks inside the dress if all else failed.

The rubbing alcohol hadn't worked, so I immediately broke

out my tiny bottle of Amodex, a stain remover for ink, and began applying it lightly with a Q-tip. Ever so slowly, the ink sank through the fabric and was absorbed by the white towel I held on the other side of the skirt. Then, to remove any oily residue from the area treated with Amodex, I applied the rubbing alcohol again.

Finally, with a laundry brush, I scrubbed the area with soap. Now the stained section was looking good, but I couldn't be sure until I had dried it with a hair dryer. Nope, a bit of the residue was still visible. I repeated the steps with the soap and brush, and then the hair dryer—just in time for the relieved bride and bridal party to walk down the aisle.

Let's complete this triad of stain stories with another special occasion—this time a baptism. Once again, my phone had rung at Mona Williams. *How late is your store open?* I told the caller five o'clock, and then we hung up. A couple of hours went by and she called again. *Are you sure you'll still be there at five?* she wanted to know. Yes, of course, I told her—but now I wanted to understand why she was so worried.

Turned out, Linda was driving nearly *four hours* to my store to bring me a century-old christening dress. Her great-grandson was about to be baptized, but she wasn't going to have him wear the gown if it couldn't be cleaned—despite the fact that he'd be the one-hundredth child to wear it. When she arrived, I understood her misgivings. Often people don't think about washing heirlooms before putting them away. Throw in the fact that babies often spit up (and do other things) all over their clothes, and you get the idea: this baptismal gown looked yellowed, at best.

Time to get to work: I mixed a tablespoon of sodium percarbonate into a large bowl of piping-hot water and gently added the gown. The yuck just floated to the surface. Progress! I then dumped out the water and started again. More bleach alternative and more water. Suddenly, the gown looked nearly as white as the day it was made. I suggested to Linda that she consider washing it by hand again before the baptism and then pressing it. A couple of weeks later I received two photos: one of her happy great-grandson in a gorgeous white gown and another of her husband—on his baptismal day, wearing the same dress.

On Your Mark, Get Set, Go

Thankfully, most of your stain stories won't be quite so dramatic. But even everyday clothes are important and often costly, so you don't want to cast them off simply because they have stains.

Let's begin with the three basic types of stains: oily, organic, and inorganic. **Oily stains** include, obviously, any kind of oil, such as vegetable, olive, and motor. What makes a particular substance an oil? According to *Merriam Webster's*, oil is "any of numerous unctuous combustible substances that are liquid or can be liquefied easily on warming, are soluble in ether but not in water, and leave a greasy stain on paper or cloth." That's a whole lot of scientific mumbo-jumbo, but all we are concerned with is that last part—about how oil stains cloth.

Organic stains originate from living organisms, and include blood ("Out, damn'd spot!"), berries, and grass, while **inorganic stains**—like mascara and cherry Kool-Aid— are manufactured items. All of this

seems pretty straightforward, and their stain solutions tend to be, too.

But stain removal becomes more complicated with stain subcategories. Let's take beets. Beets are obviously organic and, therefore, steamed beets can make an organic stain. But let's say I fry up some beets with garlic, red onion, and beet greens (also all organic) in butter—my favorite way to cook that particular vegetable. Now, when a large bite falls off my fork and lands on my shirt, I have an oily organic stain.

Or let's say you wear foundation makeup— the color in foundation makes it inorganic. But the pricier it is, the more likely it includes oil, and that makes it an oily inorganic product that can create an oily inorganic stain.

For these more complex stains, I offer other solutions, often two or even three steps, which first get rid of the oil and then remove the color (whether organic or inorganic).

But regardless of the type of stain, the most important thing is that you're going to conduct this stain removal not right when the stain happens, but immediately before washing the garment. As a rule, I don't pretreat stains. I treat stains right before I throw the items into the wash—when the vinegar-water mixture, the soap, the bleach alternative, etc., are busy at work.

Before I share the stain-removal how-tos, let's get some common questions out of the way.

What if you don't know what caused the stain? Understanding the origin of a stain means you'll know exactly how to remove it. But what if you have no idea? What if you're doing your family's laundry and you find a stain of questionable origin? *Is it grass or is it crayon?* No worries—just start with the most basic of stain-removal steps, using rubbing alcohol, and then add on other elimination methods if the first one doesn't work.

Does the type of fabric affect the stain-removal solution? In other words, does it matter if the red wine stained a silk blouse or jeans? How about lobster butter sauce on linen napkins or your nicest T-shirt? Nope, it doesn't matter at all. Whatever the fabric, you'll remove the stains in the same way and then wash as normal.

What if a stain remains after treating and washing? Before throwing a previously stained item into the dryer, make sure that the stain is completely gone. If it's not, just treat and wash again. (Pro tip: This is yet another reason to line-dry—drying on a clothes rack won't set the stain like a dryer does.)

What if you're headed out the door when the stain occurs and you need to remove the stain fast? If there's no time to treat the stain and then wash and dry the garment, you've still got a trick up your sleeve. Add rubbing alcohol to a cotton makeup pad and then, pressing and lifting, use the pad on the stain. Repeat as necessary with a new pad. Using rubbing alcohol won't leave a ring on your garment and it removes the stain about 80 percent of the time.

Stain-Removal Supplies and How-Tos

Let's get started with a reminder of the supplies needed for stain removal, as detailed at the start of the book:

☺ A bottle of bleach alternative (100 percent sodium percarbonate); use one tablespoon sodium percarbonate to one quart of water (this solution lasts roughly an hour—then it off-gasses the extra oxygen molecule and the H_2O_2 becomes H_2O, or plain water)

⊕ A small laundry brush (my favorite features horsehair)

⊕ A laundry soap bar (used with the laundry brush for spot-cleaning and found at most grocery stores), such as Fels-Naptha

⊕ A spray bottle that you've filled with 50 percent white vinegar and 50 percent water

⊕ A store-bought bottle of 70 percent rubbing alcohol (isopropyl alcohol)

⊕ A bottle of an oil-based stain solution, such as The Laundress Stain Solution

⊕ A small bottle of Amodex—magical, nontoxic stuff recommended even by permanent-ink manufacturers

⊕ A small spray bottle of cheap vodka (it's for your laundry, I promise)

⊕ Inexpensive, white terry washcloths (I buy stacks of them)

⊕ Cotton makeup pads

Following are the four most popular stains (as suggested by my thousands of Laundry Campers), my step-by-step instructions for their removal, and a few stories along the way.

Lipstick: From baby pink to fuchsia, rose to ruby, cocoa to bronze, and lavender to plum, lipstick is one of the toughest stains to remove. Granny Dude was famous for her incredibly bright red lipstick. She began wearing it when she first started putting on makeup and never stopped. It was her signature color.

Today, lipstick has become even harder to eliminate due to smudge-proof formulations, which feature more pigment and oil. Unfortunately, the more staying power a lipstick has on your lips, the more it has on your clothes, too.

To remove this oily inorganic substance, place a white washcloth underneath the stain and then generously spray the stained area with a mixture of vinegar and water. Now blot with a cotton makeup pad to remove the excess oil. Next, gently scrub the stained area with your laundry brush, which you've wetted with water and then dragged over the bar of laundry soap. Repeat the whole process a couple of times as needed, flipping over your white washcloth as you go to use a clean area to soak up the stain, and then throw the garment into the wash.

Red wine: People panic about spilling red wine—even if it hasn't landed on white cashmere or white carpet. At my house, if you spill a glass of pinot, the only thing I'm going to do is pour you another glass. (Remember: For those of us in our forties or older, drinking red wine is like a visit to the cardiologist. You're welcome.)

After the party, the next morning, or maybe even a couple of days later, I'll get around to removing the stain. Despite its reputation, a red wine stain is easy to get rid of.

To eliminate this organic stain from a garment, mix a tablespoon of sodium percarbonate in a bowl of very hot water. Now dip the stained portion of the item into the bowl, give it a swish (the stain should change color), and throw it into the wash. That's it. (To clean carpet stains—red wine and otherwise—see page 103.)

Barbecue sauce: When it comes to my mom's barbecue ribs (recipe, page 169), they're well worth any stain. She cooks her country-style ribs in the oven, and then—when they're nearly done—she brushes them with barbecue sauce and finishes them on the grill to caramelize. They're so good they're obscene. Once, I made fifteen pounds of them for a *Nine to Five*–themed dinner party for ten guests. There were no leftovers. (Remember how much Violet, Judy, and Doralee loved barbecue?)

That said, barbecue sauce is among the toughest stains to remove and likely requires three steps. To eliminate this oily organic stain, you first need to get through the bubble of oil to reach the color—remember oil and water don't mix. Generously spray the stained area with a mixture of vinegar and water. Next, scrub the area with your laundry brush and laundry soap. By now, most of the stain should be gone. Finally, to remove any remaining color from the stain, you may need to dip and swish the stained area in a bowl of bleach alternative and hot water. Then throw the garment in the washing machine and wash as normal.

Perspiration: This is my number-one most-requested stain how-to. And no wonder—yellowed underarm stains are a nearly universal annoyance. I'll not only tell you how to remove them but how to ensure you'll never have to deal with them again.

For these oily organic stains—human sweat glands in the armpits secrete an oily, smelly compound—you need to use an oil-based stain solution. Place a few drops directly onto each underarm stain. Then sprinkle the tiniest bit (maybe ten grains) of sodium percarbonate onto each dollop of solution and rub in with your finger. Let this mixture set for thirty minutes. Go for a walk, write a note to your congressperson, or Hula-Hoop. When

the time is up, pour (carefully so you don't burn yourself—I use a tea kettle) nearly boiling water right through the stain. Then throw the shirt into the wash. (This trick also works for ring-around-the-collar and stained cuffs, whose perspiration stains, similar to underarm stains, include myriad minerals, lactic acid, urea, and dead skin. The oil-based stain solution lifts the oil, and then the sodium percarbonate works on the minerals and dead skin.

Now for the really amazing trick: After removing the perspiration stains from this shirt, *every time* you wash it in the future—immediately before you wash it—spray it generously with a mixture of vinegar and water to neutralize the pH of the stain. And there you have it—you'll never have underarm stains again! You can use the same process with a brand-new shirt: The first time you wash it, spray the underarms with a mixture of vinegar and water right before you wash. Doing so will prevent underarm stains in the first place; then repeat this every time you wash.

. . . .

Removing Phantom Stains

Have you ever put an item into the dryer and then discovered a light brown stain after drying? These phantom stains occur when a bit of sugar—from fruit juice or ketchup, for example—remains on the garment after washing. The sugar caramelizes in the dryer and, unfortunately, shows up as a stain.

To remove a phantom stain, I suggest using the same process recommended for removing perspiration. Place a few drops of an oil-based stain solution directly onto the stain. Then sprinkle a bit of sodium percarbonate onto the solution, rub in with your finger, and let this mixture set for a half hour. Finally, pour nearly boiling water (ever so carefully) right through the stain. After washing once more, the stain should be gone.

* *

Now that we've got the four most-requested stain how-tos out of the way, read on for specific stain-removal methods for nearly seventy foods, household items, and more. Using these tips, you can eliminate practically every stain—lengthening the life of your garments and freeing you up to buy the clothing you love without worry.

Before getting started, keep these tips in mind:

1. If you're running out the door or you're at work and you spill something on your shirt or pants, your first go-to is rubbing alcohol. (After all, you likely don't have time to run a wash.) Simply hold a towel on the inside of the garment while spraying or applying rubbing alcohol on the stain. This will work roughly 80 percent of the time, and the rubbing alcohol will not leave a ring on your garment. (I'd suggest keeping a small bottle of rubbing alcohol handy at work, just for this purpose.)

2. If the rubbing alcohol approach doesn't work on your particular stain, use whatever method I suggest below and then launder. When you use rubbing alcohol, you're just trying to quickly remove the stain and avoid washing the garment. Why don't I recommend using rubbing alcohol to remove every stain? Because it doesn't always work and it can be more expensive than the methods detailed below.

3. When you use a method listed below, do so immediately before laundering. You want these cleaners— vinegar, sodium percarbonate, etc.—to be working as your laundry starts the wash cycle. Pretreating (even an hour before washing) doesn't work.

4. Most of the stain-removal processes below can be used on carpet. The difference is that you don't have the luxury of pouring water through the stain when needed, and you can't throw the carpet into the wash. Instead, once you've treated the stain, I recommend using a carpet cleaner/extractor if you have one. If not, soak a clean towel in warm water and press down on the stain; then fold and flip the towel as it soaks up the stain, always using a clean section of the towel to absorb more. Finally, if needed, retreat the stained area and blot again with a freshly soaked towel. Once the stain is gone, blot the area with a dry towel.

And now, in alphabetical order, here's a list of stains you may someday face and wish to remove. As always, if directions include washing, place in the correct load—whites, darks, cool colors, warm colors, or activewear:

Avocado: If you have an avocado toast or avocado smoothie incident, no worries. Just scrape off any residue with a butter knife, and then scrub the stain with your laundry brush, which you've wetted with water and then dragged over the bar of laundry soap. If there's any color left, dip the stain in a bucket or sink filled with a solution of bleach alternative and water, and then launder.

Baby formula: Plenty of parents, grandparents, and baby-sitters are walking around with this stain, but they don't need to be. This organic stain generally comes right out with laundry soap and a brush. If it doesn't, dip the stain in a bucket or sink filled with a solution of bleach alternative and water, and then launder.

Baked beans: Everyone has his or her own recipe for baked beans. I make my mom's beans, which are brown-sugary. Regardless of your favorite recipe, when you get a baked beans stain, you'll first need to cut the oil of this oily organic stain by spraying with your bottle of vinegar and water. Then scrub with laundry soap and a brush. If any color remains, just repeat the steps, and launder.

Barbecue sauce: See info on page 100.

Berries: Blackberries grow wild in Eastern Kentucky, where I grew up. We'd eat them as we picked them, but Granny Martha would freeze pints and pints of them. She was an amazing country cook, and my cousin Loretta and I would beg her to make her blackberry dumplings. However you like your berries, you can eliminate this organic stain by dipping the affected area in a solution of bleach alternative and water. Give it a swish and throw it in the wash.

Blood: Not that long ago, people used 11 percent hydrogen peroxide to eliminate lots of stains, including blood. Now, before washing, I recommend dipping the stained area (even a stain of menstrual blood) in a solution of bleach alternative and water. That's because you can no longer easily find 11 percent hydrogen peroxide. Instead, you'll likely only find 3 percent hydrogen peroxide, and that's generally not strong enough to remove most stains.

Body oil: I'm not talking lotion here, but actual body oil, produced by the human body—in other words, sweat and body grease. Dip the stain into a solution of bleach alternative and the hottest possible water. Then launder.

Butter: Corn on the cob, caramel rolls, and popcorn are just three items that are vastly improved by this delectable stuff. Thankfully, this oily organic stain is easy to get rid of. Just spray with your bottle of vinegar and water, and wash as normal.

Candle wax: Every month I get one or two requests about how to care for liturgical linens, often handmade and stained by wine, grape juice, and candle wax. See the other entries for the juice and wine. For candle wax, place the item between two layers of craft paper (a grocery bag will work just fine) and then press with a warm iron. The wax will lift right out of the fabric and be soaked up by the craft paper.

Caramel: Caramel rolls can't be beat when it comes to a special breakfast. Cancel this oily organic stain by scrubbing with laundry soap and a brush, and then launder.

Cheese sauce: Likely to happen in the stands of a stadium or in front of a TV, this oily organic stain can be scraped away with a butter knife. Then saturate the area with vinegar and water, and throw in the wash.

Chili: Thanks to the tomato in chili, this is one tough stain to remove. Spray the stained area with vinegar and water. Then scrub with laundry soap and a brush. Once the stain is mostly out, spray it again with vinegar and water to ensure there's no oil left, and wash as normal.

Chocolate: This is one of my favorite stains, because it means I got to eat chocolate—especially the killer German chocolate cake that Nancy, my wonderful stepmom, makes. While she worked as a banker, she was also a magnificent homemaker— her home is always neat, her food is always amazing, and she loves to make everyone around her happy, starting with my dad. For this oily organic stain, spray with vinegar and water, then scrub with laundry soap and a brush, and launder.

Coffee: Like seemingly all Scandinavian Americans, Marion, Ross's mom, loved coffee. She used coffee in everything—a tablespoon of coffee in gravy, a bit of coffee in her chocolate cookies to bring out the flavor, and a coffee wash brushed atop her delicious cardamom bread that she taught me to make.

No matter how you like your coffee, remove this inorganic stain (the combo of water and coffee beans makes this an inorganic dye) with laundry soap and a brush. If that isn't strong enough to eliminate the blotch, stretch the stained portion of the garment over a bowl and pour the hottest possible water through it. Pouring the water from a bit of a height—be careful, though—provides a greater force and more stain-removing power. To make that step extra easy, I just use my teakettle. After washing, make sure the stain is gone before throwing it into the dryer. If it goes through the dryer with any sugar left on it, the sugar will caramelize and a phantom stain will occur. (See "Removing Phantom Stains," page 101.)

Cranberry sauce: At Thanksgiving we always had two cranberry dishes—the cranberry sauce that comes in a can and my mom's cranberry relish. Our house was always a thousand degrees from all the cooking, so that relish, icy cold and tart, was the perfect thing to enjoy in contrast to all the heat.

Whichever cranberry dish you love, you can remove its corresponding stains by dipping the affected area in a solution of bleach alternative and hot water. Then wash.

Crayon: Just like removing candle wax, place the stained garment between two layers of craft paper (a paper grocery bag will work just fine) and then press with a warm iron. The crayon will lift right out of the fabric and be soaked up by the craft paper.

Dairy: Pretty much any dairy stain can be removed with a little sweat equity—simply scrub this organic stain with laundry soap and a brush. Then launder as usual.

Deodorant/antiperspirant: The plague of many mornings, this inorganic stain can be removed with laundry soap and a brush. Then launder as usual.

Egg: Whether sunny-side up or down, scrambled, fried, or poached, an eggy stain can be removed by scrubbing with laundry soap and a brush. Then launder as usual.

Fabric softener: If you're asking me this after reading this book, no doubt you were just using up the last quarter cup of the last bottle you'll ever own when this spill occurred. To remove this inorganic stain, throw the item into your washing machine along with vinegar, not detergent or soap, plus some washing soda (100 percent sodium carbonate).

Feces: It happens. Whether the evidence is on a diaper or a carpet, remove as much as possible and then spray the area with vinegar and water. Next, scrub with laundry soap and a brush. To sterilize, soak the item in a solution of bleach alternative and water. Finally, if the item is a textile, launder as usual.

Frosting: If your frosting has been tinted with food coloring, spray this oily inorganic stain with your bottle of vinegar and water, and then scrub with laundry soap and a brush. If it hasn't been tinted, the vinegar and water may take care of this stain on their own. Then launder.

Grass: Whether originating from gardening, building a backyard fort, or stopping a soccer goal, this organic stain can be removed by dipping the stained area into a solution of bleach alternative and water. Then launder.

Gravy: No need to worry if you've spilled this all-purpose, Thanksgiving-meal topper. Simply spray this oily organic stain with vinegar and water, and launder.

Grease: Remove this oily stain with a spritz of vinegar and water, and launder as usual.

Green vegetables: A solution of bleach alternative and water is your go-to to remove this organic stain. Then launder.

Ice cream: When I was a kid, my absolute favorite treat was a sundae of pralines and cream ice cream, topped by caramel sauce and actual pralines, at an ice cream parlor in Huntington, West Virginia. You know what? It's still my favorite.

Regardless of which ice cream is your number-one choice, you can easily remove this oily organic stain with laundry soap and a brush. If it's a fruity ice cream, you may need to swish the garment in a solution of hot water and bleach alternative as well. Launder as usual.

Ink, ballpoint: Removing ballpoint ink is a cinch. Just place a towel on the inside of the garment and spray, or blot, the area with rubbing alcohol. This inorganic stain should come right out.

Ink, permanent: Treat this inorganic stain with a few drops of Amodex. Then launder as usual.

Juice: No matter the type of juice, remove this organic stain with laundry soap and a brush. If color remains, dip the stained area in a solution of bleach alternative and water. After washing, be sure the stain is gone before throwing into the dryer. If it goes through the dryer with any sugar left on it, the sugar will caramelize and a phantom stain will occur. (See "Removing Phantom Stains," page 101.)

Kombucha: Despite the fact that people have been drinking this fermented beverage for millennia, its popularity is growing—and so are its stains. To remove this oily organic stain, spray with vinegar and water, and then dip the affected area in a solution of bleach alternative and water. Then launder.

Lipstick: See info on page 98.

Maple syrup: This brunch-y organic stain is easy to remove. Simply scrub with laundry soap and a brush and launder as normal. However, after washing, be sure the stain is gone before throwing into the dryer. If it goes through the dryer with any sugar left on the garment, the sugar will caramelize and a phantom stain will occur. (See "Removing Phantom Stains," page 101.)

Mascara: Frequently found on tops and towels, this inorganic stain is removed by spraying with vinegar and water, and then scrubbing with laundry soap and a brush. Launder as usual.

Mayonnaise: Homemade or store-bought, this popular sandwich spread creates an oily organic stain best dealt with by spraying vinegar and water, scrubbing with laundry soap and a brush, and then laundering. However, some stains may require dipping the stained area in a solution of bleach alternative and water before washing.

Mildew: Mildew is a beast to remove. The best way to eliminate mildew is to soak the stain in a solution of hot water and bleach alternative, which will kill the living mildew. Next, let the garment dry in the sun, which will kill the spores. Third, wash it. Then repeat this three-step process. During the second round, the bleach alternative solution will get rid of any remaining spores.

Mud: In springtime, "when the world is mud-luscious" and "puddle-wonderful" (thanks, e. e. cummings), turn to laundry soap and a brush to remove these delightful organic stains. Then launder.

Mustard: Turmeric is what makes this organic stain such a pain, its color often embedding itself in a garment's fibers. Before laundering, you may have to repeat these steps: First, remove as much of the mustard as possible, scraping it off with a butter knife. Second, pour hot water through the stain—I'd suggest using a teakettle. Third, scrub the stain with laundry soap and a brush. And fourth, dip the stain into a solution of bleach alternative and water. Then launder.

Nail polish: Perhaps unsurprisingly, you can remove this inorganic stain with nail polish remover. (Do not use nail polish remover on acetate, because it will melt the fabric.) Then scrub with laundry soap and a brush, and launder.

Oil (e.g., olive or vegetable): I offer the same advice as I did for butter: This oily organic stain is easy to remove. Just spray with your bottle of vinegar and water, and wash as normal.

Perspiration: See info on page 100.

Pine resin: It's no surprise that this stain tends to arise during camping season and Christmastime. Remove as much of this organic stain as possible by scraping it away with a butter knife, and then scrub with laundry soap and a brush before laundering.

Pizza sauce: Deep dish or flat, stuffed or gluten free, the type of crust is beside the point. Pretty much every pizza is topped with a tomato-based pizza sauce. To remove this oily organic stain, spray with vinegar and water, scrub with laundry soap and a brush, and then launder. (However, if the color remains after scrubbing with soap and a brush, dip the stained area in a solution of bleach alternative and water before laundering.)

Punch: My mom always made punch and now this party beverage is making a comeback. Generally, she made Wedding Almond Punch (recipe, page 168), which was red, but my favorite is orange—tart and fizzy with cranberry juice, orange juice, lemon juice, and ginger ale. She'd freeze the punch in a decorative mold and then, after placing the frozen punch into the bowl—she had various punch bowls for different occasions—she'd pour ginger ale right over the top of it. (Mom, if you're reading this, I'd really like to have your silver punch bowl—I also need the ladle.) Eliminate this organic stain by dipping the affected area in a solution of bleach alternative and water. Give it a swish and throw it in the wash. If, however, this is an inorganic stain—say, it's got added colors in one of the ingredients (Hawaiian Punch, for example)—then scrub with laundry soap and a brush, and launder as usual.

Red wine: See info on page 99.

Ring around the collar: For this oily stain, place a few drops of oil-based stain solution along the inside of the collar. Then sprinkle a small amount of bleach alternative into the solution and rub it in with your finger. Let this mixture set for thirty minutes. When the time is up, pour (carefully, so you don't burn yourself) nearly boiling water right through the stain; I use my teakettle. Then throw the shirt into the wash.

After removing the ring-around-the-collar stains from this shirt, *every time* you wash it in the future—immediately before you wash it—spray it generously with vinegar and water, and you'll never have a ring around the collar again! You can use the same process with a brand-new shirt: The first time you wash it, spray the collar with vinegar and water right before you wash it, and you'll prevent this stain in the first place; then repeat this every time you wash.

Road salt: To remove this inorganic stain, even from boots, spray with vinegar and water. For garments, launder as usual.

Rust: Squeeze fresh lemon juice right onto the stain. Do not use bottled lemon juice. Then place the garment in the sun for a few minutes. Finally, scrub with laundry soap and a brush, and launder.

Salad dressing: Spray this common, oily organic stain with vinegar and water, and then scrub with laundry soap and a brush. Launder as usual.

Sauerkraut: Whether served alongside sausages or tucked into a Reuben sandwich, this fermented cabbage condiment can stain. Scrub the affected area with laundry soap and a brush, and then launder.

Scorch: A scorch, or fabric burn (perhaps you were a little too close to the fire when roasting marshmallows), is one stain that you can't always get out, but do try. Soak for twenty-four hours in water, then scrub with laundry soap and a brush, and launder.

Shoe polish: When you're spiffing up your shoes or boots, it's not uncommon to mar a shirt cuff or the knee of your pants with a bit of shoe polish. To eliminate this oily inorganic stain, spray the area with vinegar and water, and then scrub with laundry soap and a brush. You may have to repeat these steps two or even three times before laundering.

Soda: Depending on the beverage, soda may be organic or inorganic. Regardless, you can remove this stain with laundry soap and a brush. Then launder.

Soot: Brush off as much soot as possible. Then, to eliminate this oily organic stain, first scrub with laundry soap and a brush, and then you might need to spray with vinegar and water. This is the reverse order of most stain-removal instructions. Finally, launder.

Soy sauce: Zap this organic stain in a solution of bleach alternative and water. Then launder.

Spaghetti sauce: To remove this oily organic stain, spray with vinegar and water, scrub with laundry soap and a brush, and then launder.

Sriracha/Sriracha mayo: To knock out this spicy hot sauce, increasingly used on everything, spray this oily organic stain with vinegar and water, and then scrub with laundry soap and a brush. If color remains, dip the area in a solution of bleach alternative and water. Then launder.

Sunscreen: If you dripped some sunscreen on a garment (perhaps in preparation for hanging the clothes up to dry outside), spray this oily inorganic stain with vinegar and water, and that should take care of it before laundering. Once in a while, you may need to first scrub with laundry soap and a brush before washing.

Sweet-and-sour sauce: Generously spray the stained area with your bottle of vinegar and water. Next, scrub the area with laundry soap and a brush. To remove any remaining color, dip the stained area in a solution of bleach alternative and hot water, and then launder.

Taco sauce: If evidence of your Taco Tuesday is all over your shirt, scrub the stained area with laundry soap and a brush. To remove any remaining color, dip the stained area in a solution of bleach alternative and hot water, and then launder.

Tar: To remove this tough oily organic stain, scrape off what you can with a butter knife or something dull so as not to harm your garment. Spray the stained area with vinegar and water, and then scrub with laundry soap and a brush. You may have to repeat these steps before laundering.

Tea: Black, green, or white, the type of tea doesn't matter. Remove this inorganic stain with laundry soap and a brush. If the stain remains, stretch the stained portion of the garment over a bowl and pour the hottest possible water through it. Pouring the water from a bit of height—again, be careful—provides a greater force and more stain-removing power. To make it extra easy, I use my teakettle. After washing, make sure the stain is gone before throwing it in the dryer. If it goes through the dryer with any sugar left on it, the sugar will caramelize in the dryer and a phantom stain will occur. (See "Removing Phantom Stains," page 101.)

Teriyaki: Dip the organically stained portion of this garment into a solution of bleach alternative and water, and then launder.

Tomato: I love ripe tomatoes picked fresh from the garden or purchased at a farmer's market. Add some basil, olive oil, and fresh mozzarella, and I'm practically dizzy with bliss. To remove this organic stain, dip the affected portion of the garment in a solution of bleach alternative and water, and then launder.

Turmeric: Let the organically stained portion of the garment soak in a solution of bleach alternative and water for twenty minutes, and then launder.

Vomit: So sorry that you're having to look this one up. To remove this organic stain, wipe or rinse off as much as you can. Then soak in a solution of bleach alternative and water, and launder. (And, of course, get those essential oils working for you on your wool dryer balls so that any former scent is only a memory.)

Urine: This one is super easy to remove. To eliminate this organic stain, dip the affected area in a solution of bleach alternative and water, and then launder.

Watermelon: Let me guess—you got into a major watermelon fight or at least a watermelon-seed-spitting contest. To remove any resulting stains, dip the affected area in a solution of bleach alternative and water, and then launder.

Eliminating stains is surprisingly fun, right? Now, whenever a family member asks if you can remove a particular stain, you can say, with confidence, "No problem!" Plus, you can take any spills in stride. Red wine? Barbecue sauce? Sharpie? You've got this. And don't worry about memorizing the simple how-tos. Feel free to return again and again to this comprehensive stain guide and its easy directions whenever needed.

8

Doing Better When We Know Better

Mother Earth is not a resource—she is an heirloom.
—DAVID IPIÑA,
ARTIST, POET, WRITER

Long before the film *An Inconvenient Truth*, the Paris Climate Agreement, and kids walking out of school to demand action on climate change, there was my childhood with early Earth Day celebrations, the "Keep America Beautiful" commercial (with the crying Native American portrayal), and kids and adults signing petitions to save baby seals, stop whaling, and more. Obviously, a significant percentage of us have cared about the planet's health for a long time.

But it was long before that, arguably at the beginning of the Industrial Revolution, that humans began negatively affecting our world on a wide scale. As the decades have flown past, Mother Nature has suffered significantly due to our shortsighted actions.

We're already reducing, reusing, and recycling. Now it's time for us to start renewing our laundry practices to make another major difference in our health, the health of our natural surroundings, and the health of our planet.

We Can Do Better

Caring for the environment is extremely important to me. Despite my love for clothes as a kid, I didn't hang out in the laundry room all day long—not by a long shot. I loved spending time outside.

I gardened with my parents, helping them pick out plants for our garden and my own small patch, and I especially remember waiting for the daffodils to bloom each spring. I also helped my granddad in his expansive plot, which supplied our extended family with bushels of vegetables.

But my activity in nature wasn't always so organized. Our home in Eastern Kentucky was on the top of a wooded hill. I loved meandering through the forest, collecting interesting rocks and exploring nature by myself. And when I'd visit Granny Martha and Grandpa's house many weekends, I'd splash in the creek, discovering minnows and crawdads.

When you grow up with nature at your doorstep, you take it for granted. But eventually, you realize you can no longer do that. If you truly care about this planet and the people and creatures on it, you must become a more enlightened and environmentally conscious citizen and consumer.

As best I can, I practice what I preach, teaching Earth-friendly ways to care for our clothes and supporting brands whose products are kind to the environment, my loved ones, and me. Over the years, certain practices have become automatic—using safe and plant-based soaps and detergents, avoiding products that use harmful chemicals, washing my clothes less often, hanging my textiles out to dry as often as possible, and donating and recycling clothes and shoes.

My affinity for the great outdoors is even evident in my home, where I use real twigs and moss in my décor, and furnishings such as lamps and serving pieces that feature twig and nature motifs. This aesthetic started long ago, from my connection to nature as a kid. And I still love to garden—my lime tree, brought inside during Minnesota's harsh winters, is one of my greatest joys.

But there's so much more that we can do. So let's look more closely at some environmentally focused actions relating to how we launder our clothes.

Nine Eco-Friendly Laundry Strategies

1. **Never dry clean again.** You've likely heard that dry cleaning is hard on your clothes, your health, and the environment. I'm here to suggest that you take that to heart, as all of that

is true. For more on why you shouldn't dry clean, see the next chapter.

2. Launder less. Often when an item of clothing is thrown into the wash, it doesn't actually need laundering. It simply needs a good airing out or a quick steaming to bring it back to life, or a spritz of vodka to eliminate odors, or spot treating with rubbing alcohol for that tiny risotto stain (totally worth it). These simple solutions can help your clothes look and feel as good as new without having to actually wash them. And holding off on washing saves water, energy, and time.

Have you heard of those hard-core Levi's lovers who never, ever wash their jeans? The never-wash folks make a good point when they say that washing and drying damages our garments— it's true, and that's why I highly recommend limiting washing and relying on line-drying in most cases. For these jeans fans, rather than wash their dungarees, they spot-clean stains and air out the jeans as needed. While I personally can't go that far and *never* wash my jeans—though I do wear my jeans ten or more times before I wash them—these folks are definitely on the right track.

3. Rely on Earth-friendly products. When you do wash a load, skip the fabric softeners, the dryer sheets, and those in-wash scent boosters. Stop using these toxic products and you'll no longer be spewing VOCs, including acetone and ethanol, into the air; these chemicals can harm you—and any neighbors walking by your dryer vents—causing wheezing, coughing, migraines, skin and eye irritation, and more. Plus, you won't be exposing yourself to phthalates, likely endocrine disruptors linked to damaging hormonal systems such as reproductive and developmental processes.

And for goodness sake, don't ever use bleach again.

In the washer, use high-quality, plant-based soap flakes or a liquid laundry soap that requires just a tablespoon or so per load. These are not only good for the environment, but they're so much better for your skin.

In your dryer, rely on natural, sustainable wool balls to help dry your clothes up to 40 percent faster than a load of clothes dried without them. And scent these balls, if you wish, with essential oils of your choice—perhaps citrus in the summer and frankincense in the winter. Also, don't forget to use a ball of aluminum foil to eliminate static. And get rid of stains by using such basic household products as rubbing alcohol and vinegar.

Using these nontoxic products will make your family feel good about the clothes you wear, the towels you use, and the sheets you sleep in. No doubt, you'll appreciate the fact that toxic chemicals are not touching your skin. And you'll be even happier knowing that the products you use aren't adding chemicals to your home or your community's air, water, and soil. In addition, because high-quality, plant-based soap flakes and liquid laundry soaps require so little packaging, you're creating much less to recycle—and you won't have to lug those giant plastic jugs home—or to your recycling container.

One more thought: Using environmentally friendly products can be sexy. One day a customer stopped by Mona Williams to stock up on laundry products. "For my son and for me," she said, noting that they'd both taken Laundry Camp. And then she gushed, "He just loves you." Intrigued, I asked why. Turns out her son was getting a lot of attention from young women in his college dorm—they were completely dazzled by his laundry

room prowess, his laundry products, and how good his clothes—
and he—smelled and looked.

4. **Always choose the thirty-minute washing cycle and the
fast spin.** Rely on the express cycle and you're using less water and electricity, plus you're getting better results. It's true:
Your washing machine is better able to force water through the
clothes, thereby cleaning them better, with less water in your
machine. And using a short wash cycle, rather than a long wash
cycle, delivers much less lint into the wash water and, eventually,
our waterways.

Also, the fast spin is easier on your clothes, causing less wear
and tear, than a slower cycle. It's counterintuitive, but it's true.
Think of that popular carnival ride known as the Gravitron or
the Starship, which uses centrifugal force to pin riders to the
sides of the circular drum as it spins ever faster.

The fast spin in your washing machine works the same way.
The clothes, even delicates, are pinned to the sides of the drum
as the machine empties out excess water. Now imagine if the
spin were slower: the clothes would tumble through the space,
causing abrasion and wearing out your clothes much faster.

5. **Be cool and line-dry.** Like plogging (running and picking up
trash), hanging up your clothes to dry outside is an eco-friendly
workout. I mean it's not like the calorie burn you get from hanging drywall, but hanging clothes is significantly better (consider
all that bending and reaching) than throwing those clothes into
the dryer. Plus, you're getting a nice dose of nature, including
loads of sunshine and fresh air, which boost your body's oxygen to improve concentration and amp your serotonin levels to
improve your mood. Makes you want to go hang laundry right
now, doesn't it?

Line-drying is also better for your clothes. As I noted before, nearly any quality textile can endure about fifty trips through the washer and the dryer. Skip the dryer and you've added many more washing sessions to your garments, lengthened the life of your clothes, and saved yourself a lot of money.

Perhaps most important, line-drying means you're saving energy: A clothes dryer can use as much energy per year as a "new energy-efficient refrigerator, clothes washer, and dishwasher combined," according to the Natural Resources Defense Council, a top-rated nonprofit focused on ensuring clean air, clean water, and healthy communities.

6. **Make garments last as long as possible.** Conservation laundering methods—including washing your textiles less often and line-drying more often—make your garments last longer. Imagine if that gorgeous sweater or blazer you just bought could look as good six months or a year (or more!) from now. Well, it can. Think about how much money you'll save, and how pleased you'll feel every time you pull it on. Plus, you now know how to remove stains, which means that going forward you never need to throw away a favorite garment just because it has a stain. Simply grab your stain-removing supplies and get busy.

You can take this one step further: One of my Laundry Campers was so excited about removing stains that she started shopping used-clothing stores to help her daughter build a great professional wardrobe at a fraction of the cost. She knew that if the clothes had stains, she could simply remove them! Why not follow her lead? Amazing finds are always waiting at vintage and consignment stores; and with that approach, your wardrobe won't look like anyone else's—it can represent you and your unique style.

7. **Shop thoughtfully.** Seriously consider what you buy. Do you really need another black turtleneck? Maybe not. Or how about yet another pair of jeans? And how long will that trendy short skirt be in style? Or that cowl-neck sweater?

While there's no need to be a minimalist (if you don't want to be), just weigh the value and longevity of the clothes you purchase and then enjoy the ones you do buy for as long as possible.

For example, ask yourself, "Will this item give me the value that I'm looking for?" Maybe it will. Maybe it won't. Does purchasing a high-quality item mean that you'll be buying less in the future versus buying a cheaper garment that will likely wear out faster? Or maybe you like the style, fit, and price of an inexpensive item. That's OK. Treat fast-fashion items with gentle care and they, too, can last. Just be aware of the downsides of fast fashion, and ensure that you're supporting brands that pay fairly; do their best to support safe work environments; and stamp out textile waste, water pollution, and more.

Finally, when you're absolutely done with a garment and there's no more life in it, consider recycling; many cities now offer curbside fabric recycling (including shoes). Or if the item still has some living to do, donate it to a reputable nonprofit organization, so that someone else can enjoy it. Just be sure that the items you donate are worthy of donating—would you give these same items to a friend? If not, recycle, don't donate. Another great option is to invite your friends to a clothing-swap party to extend the use of all your clothes by trading with each other for fresh looks.

When you do decide to buy a textile, consider purchasing items from makers who use natural fibers—cotton, cashmere, down, hemp, linen, and wool—all of which are renewable resources. You know by now that they're just as easy to care for as fabrics such as polyester and rayon; plus, these natural fibers break down naturally, unlike synthetic textiles that release micro-plastic fibers and pollute our waterways and oceans (see more on this in the sidebar that follows).

One more thought: The ever-so-soft fibers of cashmere (from goats) naturally offer up to eight times the insulation power of wool (from sheep) without its heavy weight. (Look at these fibers under a microscope—or check out a photo online—and you'll see a huge difference.) Thus, cashmere is better able to keep you warm but not hot. Wearing either one of these natural fibers, however, means you'll be less inclined to crank up your thermostat—yet another energy-saving measure.

. . . .

Lessening Your Plastic Output

If you wear any synthetic fabrics, and pretty much all of us do, hundreds of thousands of microscopic plastic lint fibers are released into our public waterways with every load of wash you do. Unfortunately, these fibers make up a significant percentage of plastic pollution in our oceans. They're also consumed by and harmful to marine life. Here are three things you can do to be part of the solution:

1. Strive to support manufacturers who make clothes out of natural (e.g., cotton, cashmere, down, hemp, linen, and wool), not synthetic (e.g., nylon, olefin, polyester, and rayon), textiles.

2. Every time you wash, use the thirty-minute cycle—the one I recommend for all of your loads. Short wash cycles use

less water and create less abrasion, thus releasing fewer fibers.

3. Add one or two new technologies to your laundering practices to lessen the number of plastic lint fibers released into our public waterways. Simple options include special laundry bags, in which you wash synthetic garments in order to trap microfibers, and balls, which pick up microfiber particles from your wash water (every few washes, you just clean the ball like a hairbrush, picking out the trapped lint). For a more serious approach to removing particles from wash water, consider installing a small lint filter appliance, which is attached to the back of your washing machine via hose.

. . . .

8. Use ENERGY STAR appliances. If you're in the market for a new washing machine or clothes dryer, or if your landlord is, may I suggest ENERGY STAR certified appliances? These washing machines use 25 percent less energy and 40 percent less water than regular clothes washers, and these clothes dryers use 20 percent less energy than other dryers, saving you, on average, $180 over its lifespan.

According to the U.S.-backed government energystar.gov, "If all clothes dryers sold in the U.S. were ENERGY STAR certified, Americans could save more than $1.5 billion each year in utility costs and prevent greenhouse gas emissions equivalent to those from more than two million vehicles." That's pretty darn impressive.

To save even more energy, consider an ENERGY STAR heat

pump clothes dryer. These machines use up to sixty percent less energy than a regular dryer and they operate without a heating element or a vent. That means you can install one practically anywhere, as it needs no sealing, it doesn't vent your indoor air outside, and it doesn't accumulate lint, meaning the risk of fire is much diminished. While a heat pump clothes dryer costs more than a standard dryer, these appliances save thousands of dollars in energy costs over their lifespan and go a long way toward improving our environment. Finally, while the heat pump dryer's capacity is less than a standard dryer, your clothes get a gentler drying experience, which means they'll last longer.

9. **Wash everything in one day.** While I realize I told you that I initially learned to do laundry because I wanted the freedom to wash my clothes any day I pleased, I strongly encourage washing and drying all of your household's textiles in a single day. Doing so means that all of your textiles, including your entire wardrobe, are ready to use. This gives you access to a full wardrobe that can be mixed and matched and blended together as needed, including clothes for both work and play. Having access to all of your garments allows you to own fewer things that can be worn interchangeably, and it better enables you to keep track of all the items that you own—perhaps helping you resist the itch to buy items you don't really need. Finally, establishing a single laundry day means that you don't need to think about laundry the rest of the week, and that is a gift to yourself.

Imagine what would transpire if each of us stepped up to the challenge, using only laundry methods and products that were kind to the environment. That would be an amazing transformation for us, for our communities, and for our world.

9

Special Care for Special Items

Normal is nothing more than a cycle on a washing machine.

—WHOOPI GOLDBERG,
ACTOR, COMEDIAN, AUTHOR

Like Panama hats (which actually originated in Ecuador) and pocketbooks (which are neither books nor fit in a pocket), dry cleaning is a misnomer. You can't be blamed if you thought that dry cleaning was similar to using dry shampoo—with dry-cleaning employees shaking giant containers of cornstarch onto clothes and then using small brushes to whisk away the dirt and cornstarch together.

If only dry cleaning were that simple and that environmentally conscious. But unfortunately, that's not dry cleaning at all.

The term "*dry cleaning*" simply means that it uses no water—it does, however, involve liquid. At most dry cleaners, clothes are thrown into giant commercial washing machines with a colorless liquid solvent—usually perchloroethylene, also known as tetra-chloroethylene, perc, or PCE—which is then removed before the employees press the clothes.

Unfortunately, perc is extremely hard on clothes. In fact, unlike the idea that we grew up with—that dry cleaning gently cleans our finest clothes—it's actually the opposite: machine-washing at home is better for these garments. And that's the reason I started Laundry Camp in the first place: I was concerned that dry cleaning would be far too harsh on the vintage designer clothes I sold to my customers. So I dreamed up Laundry Camp to teach them the gentler washing techniques shared in this book.

Even worse, perc is toxic to the environment. When exposed to air, it evaporates, breaking down into other chemicals, and eventually makes its way into our air, soil, and groundwater. Unfortunately, as of 2018, the EPA said it will no longer explore harms done by toxic chemicals to our air, our drinking water, our streams and lakes, or our land. In the case of perc, the EPA will only focus on harms done via actual manufacturing or when the chemical is used in dry cleaning, carpet cleaning, or certain ink-removal products.

At least that's something: According to the International Agency for Research on Cancer (part of the World Health Organization), perc is "probably carcinogenic to humans." Studies have linked it to bladder, cervix, esophagus, and kidney cancers—especially for dry-cleaning employees, those who live near dry cleaners, and people who use Laundromats that have dry-cleaning machines. In the meantime, it can also lead to other health problems, including headaches, nausea, dizziness, confusion, comas, and more.

Many groups and individuals have been working toward a perc ban—for example, Minneapolis was the first major U.S. city to eliminate the toxic chemical in 2018, and in California, dry-cleaning machines that use perc must no longer operate by 2023. Meanwhile, perc has been banned in Denmark, France, and a few other countries.

In light of the growing regulations against perc, some dry cleaners have begun using DF-2000 (isoparaffinic hydrocarbon), a petroleum-based chemical that, while less toxic, is still considered a neurotoxin (just like perc), a poisonous substance that affects the nervous system. Other dry cleaners have invested in liquid carbon dioxide, a much safer option but one that brings eye-popping dry-cleaning bills. Finally, some dry cleaners have switched to "wet cleaning," which avoids chemical solvents and uses water and detergent—just like you can do at home for much less money.

By this point in the book, you might know what I'm going to say: It's time to break up with your dry cleaner.

After all, how many times have you heard that you shouldn't be with someone who's toxic? And this toxic relationship you're in with dry cleaning might be the one that's most harmful to your life. Even if your dry cleaner employs "green" practices, this relationship is still literally costing you time and money. And for what? Anything your dry cleaner can clean, you can clean better.

It's true! You can wash nearly everything at home—even all

those supposedly dry-clean-only items, including wool suits and sheepskin boots, wedding dresses and homecoming gowns, shower curtains and pillows, and so much more. I've listed all the how-tos below—some tips courtesy of the pros who came before me, and some that emerged from my curiosity and experimentation.

That's especially true when it comes to my wool-washing method, revisited below with wool suits and wool coats. Living in Minnesota since 1999, I began indulging my sweater habit in the cold climate until my annoyance with handwashing so many sweaters finally sparked my determination to machine-wash them. I knew the trick was to prevent any abrasion during the wash cycle—hence the mesh bag and the safety pins. After experiencing success with wool sweaters—even cashmere—I soon tried machine-washing my wool suits, my wool overcoat, and much more, always using the quick-wash cycle.

So I must give credit again to Dr. Elizabeth Easter—my professor who first introduced me to alternative washing methods. And now I'm happy to share them here so that you, too, can wash nearly everything at home.

Backpack: Empty out the backpack of everything in it, including wrappers, crumbs, and any loose fibers. Then zip everything up—except for the main compartment—to protect all the flaps during the washing cycle. Leaving the main (and likely dirtiest) compartment open allows it to be thoroughly washed. Wash on the quick cycle with soap flakes or a safe, plant-based, liquid laundry soap then line-dry.

Baseball caps: Here's a fun trick: Rather than throwing your baseball caps into the washing machine, even in a mesh bag, I recommend washing them in the dishwasher! Place all of your dirty caps on the top rack of your dishwasher, allowing its various tines to hold them in place; wash them on their own with dishwashing soap during a quick-wash cycle. Then line-dry.

Bathtub mats: Bathtub mats aren't textiles, so only their surfaces must be cleaned. Soak bathtub mats in a mixture of vinegar and water, and then scrub and rinse clean.

Bath and kitchen sponges: Sponges can be thrown into a mesh bag and washed as normal in the washing machine. However, I prefer washing these, too, in my dishwasher, right along with my dishes, on the top rack.

Beds (for pets): If Buddy's bed requires laundering and it's stuffed with Poly-fil, wash as normal in either a front- or top-loading washing machine. Be sure to add a tablespoon of bleach alternative to the wash to remove any oils from your pet's coat. Then hang it up to dry. Once completely dry, fluff it up in the dryer, using the no-heat, air-fluff setting and a few tennis balls.

If Mittens's bed is filled with down, however, it must be washed in a front-loading machine; in a top loader, the bed will simply float and not get clean. If you only have a top loader, bake some cookies (or dog biscuits or cat treats) and go visit a fellow pet-lover with a front loader. Wherever you end up washing your pet's bed, add a tablespoon of bleach alternative to wash away any oils from your pet's coat. After washing, throw it in the dryer with a bunch of clean tennis balls to plump it up.

Boots (suede-sheepskin): These specialty boots (Uggs and the like) require handwashing. Begin by spraying them with an equal mixture of vinegar and water, and then gently scrub them with your laundry brush and laundry soap to remove any salt. Next, submerge the boots in a bucket, a laundry tub, or even a bathtub, to which you've added soap flakes or a liquid laundry soap. Don't use detergent, as that can negatively affect the boots' moisture-repellant treatment. Let them sit in the soapy water for about twenty minutes, rinse them clean with fresh water, and then lay them flat to dry on their sides so that any extra water runs out. Placing them in front of a fan is great, but in front of heat—no way (heat, too, can harm the moisture-repellant treatment). Be sure to fluff up the sheepskin interiors with your fingers.

Car mats: There are several ways to wash carpeted car mats. In the winter, I tend to just throw them in the washing machine and wash normally—they turn out just fine. In the summer, I wet them down with the hose in my backyard, sprinkle soap flakes on them, scrub them with a stiff brush, and then rinse. You can also do this in your bathtub. Whatever way you choose to wash your car mats, hang them on a drying rack or over your back fence to dry.

Coat (fur coat): Place the coat in your (very clean) bathtub to which you've added a few inches of warm water and soap flakes. Add the coat to the tub, gently knead the fur with your fingers for a few minutes, and then let the coat rest in the soapy water for about twenty minutes. Next, swish the coat again in the soapy water and let the water drain from the tub. Now fill the tub with fresh tepid water, and let the coat soak for another twenty minutes; then drain the tub again. For the third and final time, fill the tub again with fresh tepid water, let the coat soak again, and then drain the tub. Allow the coat to rest in the tub overnight or even for twenty-four hours. When the coat is just damp, hang to finish drying.

Coat (raincoat): Button or zip up the raincoat and then place it on your bed or a table with its front down. Fold in the sides and then the sleeves to create a long rectangle; then roll up the coat and place it in a large mesh bag, safety-pinning the mesh bag snugly around it so it can't move. Wash as normal, but use soap flakes or a liquid laundry soap, not detergent, as that can negatively affect the coat's moisture-repellant treatment.

After washing, remove the coat from the mesh bag and shake it out. While some manufacturer instructions say that machine drying is fine, I highly recommend hanging up your raincoat to dry. Again, the heat of the dryer can harm the moisture-repellent treatment. If you need to iron it, do so when the coat is still slightly damp and iron with a pressing cloth.

Coat (wool coat): Yep, you can wash a wool coat at home. I wash mine at the end of every winter and it's a doozy—black cashmere and hemmed to the floor to keep me extra warm throughout cold Midwestern winters.

First button the coat and then place it on your bed or a table with its front down. Fold in the sides and then the sleeves to create a long rectangle; then roll up the coat and stuff it into a large mesh bag.

Next, fasten the mesh bag securely around the coat with several safety pins. The goal: You don't want the coat to move within the mesh bag. Then wash the coat as normal.

After washing, remove the coat from the mesh bag, shake it out, and hang to dry, patting flat the areas that are particularly wrinkly. When the coat is still slightly damp, press as needed.

Down items: You can wash nearly any down item—including jackets, sleeping bags, and comforters—in a front-loading washing machine. Unfortunately, top loaders don't work for down garments, because they float in the water and don't really get clean. If you have a top loader, whip up some brownies or a pie and go visit a friend with a front loader. Or head to a Laundromat and eat the brownies yourself.

The real difference in caring for down garments comes in the drying process. For a comforter, throw it in the dryer with a bunch of clean tennis balls for maximally fluffed results. For the jacket or sleeping bag, however, hang to dry—the heat of the dryer is too hot for the exterior fabric. And nope, the down won't get musty if you air dry. Then, once the jacket or sleeping bag is completely dry, fluff it up by throwing it into the dryer with tennis balls on the no-heat, air-fluff setting.

Dress (prom, pageant, and wedding dresses): There's typically too much fabric to wash any of these dresses in a washing machine. Instead, head to your bathroom and place the gown—satin, sequins, tulle, and all—in your (very clean) bathtub to which you've added a few inches of warm water and some soap flakes. Now spend a few minutes gently swishing the dress through the water with your hands, and then let the dress rest in the soapy water for twenty minutes or so. Next, swish the dress again in the soapy water and let the water drain from the tub. Now fill the tub with fresh tepid water, let the dress soak for another twenty minutes, and drain the tub again. For the third and final time, fill the tub again with fresh tepid water, let the dress soak again, and then drain the tub. Allow the dress to rest in the tub for a few hours or even overnight. Finally, hang the dress to finish drying.

Feather bed: Unfortunately, you can't wash a feather bed in a residential-size washing machine. Instead, take this item to a Laundromat with commercial-size washing machines. Then wash the bed as normal and throw it in the dryer with at least a trio of clean tennis balls to fluff up the feathers.

Lunch bags: Empty out any crumbs from the fabric lunch bag, turn it inside out, and wash as normal with your regular wash. Line-dry.

Mop heads: The best way to wash a mop head is to place it in a mesh bag—to prevent tangling—and then wash it as normal. For maximal cleaning, add a tablespoon of bleach alternative right in the washer's drum. Then line-dry.

Oven mitts: While fabric oven mitts can be laundered as normal in a mesh bag in your washing machine, the easiest way to wash silicone oven mitts is to wash them in your dishwasher on the top rack. You should line-dry silicone mitts, but you can dry fabric mitts in the dryer.

Pillows: Whatever type of pillow you own—down or Poly-fil—you can wash them as normal in a front-loading washing machine. Feel free to stuff them in. If you have a top loader, however, be sure to wash an even number of same-size Poly-fil pillows (two or four, for example) so you don't throw off your machine's balance. Unfortunately, you can't wash down pillows in a top loader—they float and don't get clean. If that's your situation, it's time to get out the butter, sugar, eggs, and flour, and use the bribery, ahem, baking method shared above.

After washing, throw down pillows right into the dryer with three clean tennis balls to fluff them up. For Poly-fil pillows, hang them up to dry or place them across the top of a drying rack—the heat of the dryer is too hard on these. Then, once the Poly-fil pillows are completely dry, fluff them up in the dryer with tennis balls using the no-heat, air-fluff setting.

Stuffed animals: Whenever Teddy needs a bath, place this Poly-fil guy in a mesh bag to protect his plastic eyes and any other accessories. Then wash as normal in either a front- or top-loading washing machine. Hang him up to dry and, once he's completely dry, fluff him up in the dryer, using the no-heat, air-fluff setting and a few tennis balls.

Rugs (small): Throw small rugs right into the washing machine. Then hang to dry. I've even thrown small, inexpensive oriental rugs in the wash with good results.

Rugs (large): If it's snowy outside and you've got a rug that needs cleaning, you're in luck (if it's not snowy, see below). Here's what you do: After a fresh snow has fallen, take your area rug outside and place it faceup on an area of snow for five minutes to chill slightly. Next, flip the rug upside down on a clean patch of snow for twenty minutes. Then, flip it back over and, with a stiff broom, sweep snow onto the top of the rug; let the rug sit with the snow on it for twenty minutes before sweeping the snow back off again. The look of your rug should be much improved. Now, rather than bringing it right back into your home, let it warm up a bit in a garage or atop kitchen tile.

If, however, you're enjoying a balmy season, here's what you do: Take your area rug outside and place it faceup on a clean driveway or a large clean sheet. Spray the top of your rug with a yard hose (not a power washer), sprinkle soap flakes across it, rub the soap in with your fingers, and then rinse it off. Then flip the rug over and spray the back. Flip it back over and let the rug dry.

Running shoes and sneakers: If the shoes are fabric, place them in a mesh bag and wash as normal with your other laundry. If they're leather, however, it's best to spot treat them. If you must wash them, fill a basin with water and add a smidgen of soap; then wash by hand. Be sure to pull out the insoles and wash these separately. (Alternatively, consider just washing the insoles.) Rinse everything well and allow to air dry.

Shower curtain and liner: If your shower curtain is silver lamé, like mine, it requires placing it in a mesh bag before washing. Or maybe it's a wool blend. Then roll it up in a mesh bag and fasten securely to prevent any abrasion during a normal wash. Or maybe it's cotton—then just throw it right into the washing machine. Use your best judgment based on your shower curtain's fabric and simply wash accordingly. To clean a shower liner, wash it in your machine on its own with soap flakes or a safe, plant-based, liquid laundry soap and a tablespoon of bleach alternative to remove any scale and mildew.

Slipcovers: While I know a few Laundry Campers who wash their slipcovers in their washing machine and experience no problems, I typically just spot-clean my slipcovers. If you do decide to wash your slipcovers, wash them as normal, ensuring that you use the fast spin to get them as dry as possible. Then, rather than drying them in the dryer, I recommend zipping the slipcovers right back on your cushions while they're still damp to ensure they fit well. You can just smooth out any wrinkles with your hands. Let the pillows dry thoroughly before placing them back on your sofa.

Sports gear: To clean sports gear, from scuba equipment to curling gloves, it's best to rely on manufacturers' guidelines. Each (often pricey) item likely calls for special instructions, and this is one instance where you can follow those directions. If you're cleaning your gear at the end of a sports season, be sure to store it in a place free from dirt—or cover it with an old, clean sheet or muslin, so the gear is ready to use, and not dusty, when the right season rolls around again.

Wool suit: Begin with the suit jacket spread out on your bed or a table with its front down. Fold in the sides and then the sleeves to create a neat rectangle; fold the jacket in thirds, then roll it up, and tuck it into a medium-size mesh bag.

To avoid any abrasion while the suit jacket is washing, fasten the mesh tightly and securely with several safety pins to prevent the jacket from budging while in the washing machine. You want the suit jacket to look like a giant sausage, with the mesh bag as its casing.

Next, for the dress pants, place one leg atop the other, fold in half, and then fold in thirds—you want the pants to be folded as small as possible. Or you can place one leg atop the other and roll up the pants. Whichever method you use, place the pants in a small mesh bag and secure again with safety pins. Remember: You don't want the pants to budge. Then wash the suit with the load of clothes that makes sense for the color of your suit, e.g., a black suit with black clothes or a navy suit in a load of cool colors. Wash on warm using the thirty-minute cycle.

After washing, take the jacket and pants out of the mesh bags, shake them out, and hang to dry, patting flat the areas that are particularly wrinkly. When the garments are nearly dry, press as needed.

(Pro tip: As I've mentioned before, unless it's the victim of a spill, a wool suit likely only needs to be washed once a season. In the meantime, just air it out.)

Yoga mat: Like bathtub mats, yoga mats aren't textiles, so only their surfaces must be cleaned. For a great yoga mat cleaner, mix equal parts vinegar and water in a small spray bottle, and then add a few drops each of two antibacterial essential oils (tea tree, lavender, or eucalyptus are good choices). Simply spray and wipe.

Now that you've completed this chapter on caring for special items, I hope you're inspired, already thinking about favorite garments in the back of your closet that you've been meaning to dry clean. Who needs dry cleaning when you can launder everything you own at your home, in your apartment or dorm laundry room, or in a Laundromat! Not only will you be treating your garments (and yourself) more gently and more responsibly, you'll be saving lots of time and money, too. Unlike your wash loads, the benefits of home laundry just keep piling up.

10

Making the Laundry Room Your Happy Place

I used to have a blankie, and when my mom had to
wash it, I would sit outside the dryer and watch it go
round and round, and cry.

—DREW BARRYMORE,
ACTOR, DIRECTOR, PRODUCER,
ENTREPRENEUR

Flip through home magazines or surf online through gorgeous
laundry room images and it's easy to imagine blissful washing-
and-drying sessions performed in a space outfitted with crystal
chandeliers, cabinets with wainscoting, a dog-washing station,
a wine cellar, and a hot tub.

Sound like your laundry room? Not mine, either. While few

of us are that fortunate (and perhaps we don't even aspire to have dominion over such a room), most laundry rooms could stand to have some better organization, a couple of items to improve our laundering efficiency, and some cheery decor.

And that's if your laundry room is under your own roof. But what if you use an apartment laundry room, a dorm laundry room, or a Laundromat? How can you add more fun to your laundry room experience—regardless of what type of facility you use?

That's what this chapter is all about. But before we get down to brass tacks (or clothespins, as it were) and I share a few insights, plus great tools and tips, I'd like to give you a tour of the laundry room of my dreams.

This laundry room doesn't feature a sauna, a sensory deprivation tank, or a clothes-folding robot (although that would be awesome). My wants are much more down-to-earth and far more fun.

To begin, my dream laundry room (like my current one) would be next to my bedroom for short trips back and forth with my clothes, bedding, and towels. Two washers and one dryer would offer maximal time efficiency. A steam cabinet, common in department-store backrooms, would make garment steaming a cinch. A built-in drying rack would disappear into a custom cabinet and, of course, a hanging rod would accommodate lots of drying shirts.

A jetted laundry sink—like a whirlpool bath for clothes—would let me wash a single item or two, plus I could use it to see whether my stain-removal steps have gone far enough before throwing an item into my washing machine. (Also, I would totally climb up on the counter and stick my feet in the laundry tub for a jetted foot soak.)

I'd have a bar sink for washing my hands while something soaks in the other sink and a mini fridge stocked with Diet Coke (and gin for the occasional G&T). A built-in sound system would spark some grooving as I fold and could lead to spontaneous dance parties. And one main item that I'd retain from my current laundry room is a disco ball. (Like hangers, a disco ball is a must in every laundry room.)

A spacious ironing area would accommodate the ironing board—permanently set up and ready to go on a moment's notice. A generous-size island would enable clothes folding on one end and spot-treating on the other, while canvas laundry bins would roll right underneath. Bright lighting, including at least one window, would enable me to see well enough to hem a pair of pants or sew on a button in the sewing area. And a couple of chairs (laminate for easy cleaning) would let us catch our breath after all that dancing. (Of course, friends are invited to join in on the laundry fun.)

Speaking of dancing, the natural (and nontoxic) linoleum floor would be heated so that our tootsies would always be warm, no matter the season or time of day. And toe-kick vacuum vents, just like in a hair salon, would enable quick and easy vacuuming for a spick-and-span space. Finally, I'd draw a line at adding a TV. Because if I did, I may never leave my dream laundry room.

(Truth be told, I'd also love to have a small washer and maybe even a dryer near my kitchen for loads of tablecloths, linen napkins, and kitchen towels. OK, now I'm done dreaming.)

Back to Reality

The worst laundry room I ever used was one in college that had the washer and dryer on opposite sides of the room. And it had no sink. Doing laundry there was a total pain. The most amazing laundry room I ever actually set foot in was a former breakfast room in a beautiful home. Green palm-print wallpaper ensconced one wall, classic black-and-white tiles covered the floor, and three walls of windows looked out over a horse ranch.

But for sheer efficiency, my favorite room to do laundry in is at my mom's house. Unlike the one that I grew up using, this laundry room features refurbished kitchen cabinets for lots of storage, a large table in the middle of the room for folding clothes and removing stains, and a rod that runs the room's length for hanging clothes. Doing laundry there is simple and easy. And when I have my mom there to keep me company, how could it not be fun?

Most of us inherit our laundry rooms when we move into our homes, whether single-family dwellings or apartments. For many of us, the laundry room is more of a closet, with stackable appliances hidden behind a door. For others, the laundry room is in a dark, unfinished basement with a cobwebby ceiling and a bare lightbulb lit with the pull of a chain (like the creepy laundry room in *Home Alone*). And for lucky others, it's a combination mudroom-laundry room, which allows dirty clothes to go right into the washer. No matter what your laundry room looks like, even if it's one of those glossy-magazine-type laundry rooms, a few improvements can up your laundry game and your laundering experience.

Soon my friend Mary Ann will move into a brand-new condo. She's one of the fortunate few who didn't inherit her laundry room but gets to design it. In fact, when she found out that the builder was inviting her input on its layout, she turned to me for advice. I, of course, was only too happy to help.

As originally designed, hers is one of those hallway laundry rooms—really, more of an alcove—hidden behind folding doors. My goals? To maximize its space, to ensure it serves all of her laundry needs, and to make it fun. For starters, I recommended using a stackable washer and dryer. That way Mary Ann has space to add a small laundry sink, enabling her to remove stains right there (not in her kitchen or bathroom sink). I also suggested hanging a bar over the sink to accommodate drying laundry. Next, I advocated replacing the folding doors with a solid wood door so that she can add an accordion-style laundry rack to the inside. And I proposed a small counter on which she can remove stains and fold clothes. Lastly, I advised painting the wall a bright pop of color and including a piece of artwork to set an upbeat tenor for all the tasks performed there. (I didn't suggest hanging a disco ball—that's because I want to bring her the perfect housewarming gift.)

So how can you improve your laundry room? Well, that depends on your space, but I have a bunch of ideas:

1. **If you have any say in the matter, buy an efficient washing machine.** People always ask me what type of washing machine to buy. If your washing machine dates back to 2003 or earlier, it's time to consider upgrading to a high-efficiency (HE) model. The HE designation means that it uses less water, less electricity, and less

soap than a traditional washing machine. Next, make sure that you're only looking at ENERGY STAR models. This certification ensures that these machines have a greater tub capacity, according to energystar.gov, allowing you to wash fewer, larger loads; plus, they use 25 percent less energy and 40 percent less water. Once you've checked those two boxes, confirm that the machine you purchase has three features that you can control: temperature, spin speed, and the number of minutes a wash runs. If your machine can do all this, you're A-OK. (If your dryer has seen better days, consider upgrading your dryer as well. For more on energy-efficient dryers, see page 125.)

2. **Turn up your lighting.** There's no need for you to be doing laundry like a prisoner in a dark dungeon. If you lack a window and its inherent natural light, contemplate using daylight bulbs via track lighting, flush-mount fixtures (mounted right below your ceiling), or can lights (which disappear into the ceiling). By illuminating every corner, you suddenly won't feel like fleeing the room; plus, sorting clothes, finding and treating stains, sewing on buttons, and all laundry-related tasks will be that much easier to perform. And don't forget about adding a table lamp or under-cabinet lights for such tasks as treating stains or sewing on buttons; LED bulbs with a rating near 100 will provide a comfortable light. If the laundry room you use is not your own, consider discussing these and other potential improvements with the powers that be at your apartment building or college dorm.

3. **Get organized.** Each bedroom should have a laundry hamper, preferably one that can by carried by its handles. If a hamper can't be carried, transfer dirty clothes to the laundry room or Laundromat via a laundry basket or bag.

   Ideally, you'll wash all of your textiles on a single day, but that may not always happen. If you've got the space—say, you live in a single-family home—and your bedroom hampers are often overflowing, consider adding rolling laundry-sorting canvas bins to your laundry room; mark each with a sorting category: whites, blacks, cool colors, warm colors, and activewear. Doing so, especially if you have a household of three or more individuals, means that your loads are ready to wash whenever you are. Finally, once everything has been washed, dried, and folded, use the laundry baskets, bags, or hampers to return items to your home or to your bedrooms. Or simply carry the clothes in your arms to your bed, where you fold everything (of course, it helps that my bedroom is right next to my laundry room).

4. **Make it functional.** If you use a Laundromat, you've already got oodles of washing machines and dryers at your disposal—super functional. That's especially true if you choose a less-busy time to get your laundry done. Land four machines simultaneously and you're headed home in no time.

   But, if you have your own laundry room, you can make a big difference in the time you spend there by boosting its functionality. For example, if you have a sink in your laundry room, you can certainly get by with a standard faucet—but having a high-tech one, including a pullout head for filling buckets and a spray feature for helping to remove stains, makes a nice upgrade. For storage, if you have the space, consider adding kitchen cupboards or open shelving, and invest in bamboo, natural straw, or water hyacinth woven baskets—all good, environmentally friendly choices—that look beautiful and work just as hard as any plastic baskets. To ensure you line-dry as often as possible, outfit your laundry room with at least one drying rack. Consider a freestanding design or, if you're tight on space, wall-mounted models that feature accordion racks or multiple swing-out arms; these fold flat against the wall when not in use. (These are also a great option, perhaps tucked away in a closet or pantry, for folks who often handwash and need a place to dry a few items.) A rolling rack is another good option; it lets you hang up clothes to dry or store during an off-season. I suggest ordering yours from an industrial supplier—most run less than $100. Or you can install a hanging rod for the same purpose. Finally, a small counter, placed atop your washer and dryer, makes a nice folding table in a pinch; or if you have more square footage, a folding table is ideal for folding clothes and removing stains.

5. **Add a bit of whimsy.** Life can get pretty serious. So it's great to be able to set most of your worries aside while accomplishing a task like laundry—especially if you're doing so in a playful place. Why not get creative

with paint? If your laundry room is your own, consider painting a border around your hopper windows, an underwater scene on your walls, a bright color on your floor, or a blue sky and a couple of fluffy clouds on your ceiling. Or add a mural, perhaps with a colorful geometric design or some serene nature element, to your space.

Last summer a friend applied peel-and-stick wallpaper of classic white subway tile to her laundry room's drywall—and suddenly the space looked brighter and better than ever before. Fortunately, even renters can use peel-and-stick wallpaper. Moving out? Just remove the wallpaper that you enjoyed so much while the apartment and its laundry room was yours.

You can also add art to the space. While the trend is to hang a sign that says "Laundry Room," I'm guessing everyone in your household knows what the room is for. How about an actual print, a framed favorite poster, or a fanciful sculpture? One Laundry Camper placed a hedgehog sculpture in her laundry room's window. There are no limits to what you can select. Just choose something that you love and will continue to enjoy every time you do laundry.

6. **Make your escape.** Need a space to call your own—or even a hideout? If you've got kids under age eight, it's likely you don't even go to the bathroom by yourself. As long as you've got another adult caring for the kids, I've got a fix: Announce that you're headed to the laundry room or Laundromat, and I'm guessing no one will follow you there. The key to this plan is keeping to yourself just how much fun laundry is! Then make the

experience your own: Add an aromatherapy diffuser, a table lamp or a Himalayan salt rock light, a throw rug you can sink your toes into, perhaps a yoga mat. Don't own your laundry room? You can still level up the experience—pack your favorite magazine or current book, chocolate, a beverage, and some tunes. Then, while the machines are a-rocking, grab some well-deserved time for you!

You get the idea. Transforming this space—stereotypically known to be underwhelming and sometimes even depressing—will make laundering all the more enjoyable. After all, this is the room where you spend a good deal of time showing your love for others by caring for their clothes, bedding, and more. Making it nice for you makes it all the more conducive to doing something nice for others.

Top Ten Reasons to Love a Laundromat

Having clean clothes is a luxury. And while there are downsides to doing laundry in a shared facility (e.g., jockeying for machines, using a washer that's very familiar with fabric softener, and literally airing your dirty laundry in public), there are lots of upsides, too—even for people who have their own laundry rooms. Let's count them down.

10. Most Laundromats boast a bevy of windows, which can make the space inviting and ideal for tasks in need of good light, such as sorting and stain removal.

9. At a Laundromat, you can wash and dry those bulky items (down comforter, I'm looking at you) that require a front-loading machine. Plus, as I mentioned before, with numerous washing machines and dryers at your disposal, it's likely you can run multiple loads at one time—talk about a time-saver!

8. When you're on vacation, where else can you launder your clothes and mingle with locals, from whom you might learn about the best hole-in-the-wall restaurant or a great playground for the kids?

7. Undistracted by other household chores, you can relax while your clothes tumble through the machines. Bring along a throw, a favorite book, and a fancy coffee and you've got the makings of a great afternoon.

6. On the other hand, why not make it a date or a gabfest? Invite a friend or two to join you, pack snacks and beverages, and launder while you socialize. In college, my friend Bethany and I stayed caught up by hitting the Laundromat at the same time every week. Doing laundry is all the more fun when you do it together! (A dear friend to this day, Bethany is totally a "handwash cold, dry flat" type.)

5. Take advantage of the Laundromat's amenities. Most provide free Wi-Fi, magazines, and TVs. A rare few are complete show-offs, offering coffee bars, actual bars, free pizza, and even hairstyling services.

4. Have children? A Laundromat is an endlessly fascinating place for kids, packed with rows of giant machines filled with water and spinning clothes. They're like screens, only better. Plus, many shared laundry facilities feature kids' play and reading areas. And a change of scenery is often great for the whole family.

3. Writing a book? Finishing your master's in sociology? Beefing up your photography portfolio? Any of these reasons and many more might draw you to a Laundromat, where the people watching can't be beat.

2. What's better than people watching? Some days it's people chatting. You can hear interesting conversations in a Laundromat, but why not join in? Pretty much everyone is there for the same reason, so you're likely to have other things in common as well.

1. Doing all of your laundry in one session is exactly what you do at a Laundromat—and that's what I recommend. No need to go there twice in a single week. Pack up all of your textiles plus a backpack or a reusable shopping tote with all your supplies: soap flakes or a safe, plant-based, liquid laundry soap stain-removing gear; wool balls; essential oils; and an aluminum foil ball. These days, you might not even need to bring quarters—most Laundromats offer change machines, and many washing machines and dryers allow you to pay with your phone. You're good to go!

. . . .

Kids in the Laundry Room

At Mona Williams, I carry child-size brooms. That's because I believe kids want to contribute to their family's happiness and that they gain satisfaction from a job well done. The same is true of caring for clothes.

Even young children can start learning these skills. Toddlers, for example, can remove their clothes by themselves and place them into a laundry hamper. Better yet, teach children to hang up their clothes after wearing, and that prevents a whole bunch of nearly clean clothes from needing another wash.

Once children are a little older, invite your kids to help put away freshly laundered textiles, teaching which items are tucked into drawers and which items are hung on hangers. A simple system and plenty of storage space help ensure that children are successful. Consider placing the closet rod low so that kids can reach it easily, and ensure any drawers close slowly to avoid pinched fingers.

When the kids hit their tweens, invite them to start helping out in the laundry room, loading the washer and dryer, and helping to fold the clothes. Depending on the kid, you'll know which skills to introduce. And while some chores—such as cooking a multicourse dinner without any help—are beyond most kids at this age, they can be successful launderers all on their own.

Finally, ensure that they're doing the family's laundry and not just their own. Learning about the joy of service to others should start early.

. . . .

I hope you come away from this laundry-room chapter bursting with new ideas to improve your overall laundry experience—whether it regularly takes place in a plain-Jane or fancy-schmancy laundry room, a shared basement laundry, or your friendly neighborhood Laundromat. As I've said before, doing laundry should be fun! And don't forget the disco ball.

11

Better Laundry Leads to Better Shopping

I feel like I should be able to wear what I want, when
I want, however many times I want.

—TIFFANY HADDISH,
ACTOR, COMEDIAN, AUTHOR

Second to textiles in this life, I love Christmas. I love everything about it: I love decorating for Christmas (every room in
my house features a Christmas tree with themed decorations).
I love buying Christmas presents, selecting the perfect thing for
each family member and friend (January is not too early to start
shopping). I love cooking for Christmas, especially my mom's
sugar cookies, Granny Dude's Blue Cheese Spread (recipe, page

168), and Roberta's Bourbon Balls (recipe, page 173). And I love celebrating Christmas with my family and friends.

So it's no wonder that my first-ever outing as an infant was with my Granny Dude (giving my tired mom a break), who took me to the annual Christmas parade in Grayson, Kentucky, and a local boutique where she bought me an adorable outfit. Of course I was introduced to shopping and Christmas, my two favorite things, in one fell swoop when I was only weeks old.

Little did Granny Dude or I know just how much shopping we were going to do together after that first outing. We shopped—a lot—and often with my mom. I don't even have a memory of going back-to-school shopping, because we were always shopping, anytime of the year. Not that we always bought something—we were browsers as often as we were buyers.

Of course, when Granny Dude was growing up, no dry cleaner did business in her small town. She just figured out how to care for her clothes on her own and wore whatever she wanted. She was brave in her fashion choices, but she was never afraid of the care they required.

This is the first fashion lesson I learned from Granny Dude: When no item of clothing is off-limits to purchase, it's much more fun to go shopping. As long as you can afford it, you can buy whatever you love without worrying about overbearing fabric instructions.

All of the updated laundry skills you now have give you a new lease on shopping. In terms of fabric care, no article of clothing is off-limits anymore. A Laundry Camper was telling me how her daughter had whispered her admiration for a light blue wool coat worn by a woman passing by. But then she added, "It would show dirt so quickly, though, and dry cleaning is so expensive." The mom was delighted to inform her daughter that she could, in fact, buy a coat like that, and she'd be glad to teach her how to care for it.

Remember when you saw that special item hanging in that shop downtown, or in your favorite department store, or perhaps in that little boutique on your last vacation? You were attracted to it and you wanted to buy it, but you walked away because you thought it would be too hard or too expensive to care for. Now you realize just how wrong you were, because caring for clothes is easy once you know how.

The second important fashion lesson Granny Dude taught me was this: Wear everything you own. That sounds intuitive, but it's often not. What I mean to say is that there's no reason to save special items for occasions that never seem to come. Don't have a black-tie gala on your calendar? (Few of us do.) Then throw on your tuxedo jacket over a T-shirt and jeans and head to a fast-food joint. Don't have a hot date this weekend? Then wear that darling dress to the grocery store. I'm giving you permission right now to have more fun every day with fashion.

A Trio of Cardigans

As someone who has worked in designer fashion for more than two decades, I understand a lot about shopping and I know how to create individual looks for my clients. I'm glad to share a few of my secrets here.

To begin, I confess that I hate those articles that tell you what you should own—e.g., "The ten wardrobe essentials you need." Just because those work well for one person doesn't mean they'll work for everyone. We all live unique lives, with individual interests, and in wide-ranging geographies. Minimalist wardrobes work for very few people—perhaps forest rangers, marine biologists, and nudists. For the rest of us, a minimalist approach seems like a great idea until your job requires you to attend a far-flung conference, or your niece invites you horseback riding, or your best friend gets tickets to an all-day music festival. Suddenly those ten pieces seem lacking.

All to say, there's not one right way to do a wardrobe. In addition to basic items that best serve your life, I'd suggest buying a few garments that you really want in the colors you really love—then figure out how to make them work with the rest of your apparel. Maybe you don't have anything to go with that orange cashmere jacket—but maybe you do. Be open to possibilities.

Personally, I've always had a thing for cardigans. I think it goes back to my granddad. He constantly wore cardigans and owned them in probably a dozen colors. In fact, Granny Dude told me that only once, at their wedding, did her husband ever wear a suit. Otherwise, his daily uniform comprised a shirt, a pair of trousers, and a cardigan.

A cardigan just makes sense to me: It's easier to move in than a jacket, and it's the perfect thing to pull on if you get chilly or to remove if you're too warm. Living in Minnesota, where the weather can change on a dime, I find the cardigan to be the perfect garment.

In fact, the most luxe item in my closet is a cardigan. Roughly a decade ago, I was working at Nordstrom when designer Zang Toi arrived for a special trunk show. I pulled out a woman's wrap and immediately fell in love with its extraordinary fabric. Black-and-white herringbone cashmere, it was embroidered with delicate branches of cherry blossoms. I had to have it and, because I love cardigans, I asked Zang if he'd consider making me one using this spectacular fabric. He agreed and this amazing garment was in my hands in just weeks. Yet despite its price—or maybe because of it (I will go to my grave not telling anyone what I spent)—I wear it often and everywhere. In fact, I'm surprised I haven't worn it out. I love it so much.

Now let me tell you about another cardigan. It's the Coogi cotton cardigan, circa 1995, that should be folded and put away with my other sweaters. Unfortunately, despite how much I love these colorful sweaters, I've never found the right one to buy. When they were first popular, I sold them at McAlpin's department store. Even when they fell out of favor, and then again when they came back in style, I continued to search. To this day, every once in a while, I look online for a vintage Coogi cotton sweater. I know there's one out there for me. I'm just holding out for my ideal.

And then there's shopping destiny—like my first-ever trip to New York, where I walked into a Polo store and found the cardigan that I'd been told over the phone was sold out. They had one left and it was in my size.

So what's your version of a cardigan? Is it a great blazer? A beautiful blouse? A stunning pair of shoes? Keep that in mind when you shop. Perhaps you own a couple of great jackets, but now, understanding how you can care for blazers at home, you can add a truly noteworthy one to your closet.

Again, be open to newness. Sometimes it's fun to spring for something outside your comfort zone. People are too afraid to make mistakes in their clothing choices, but doing so is never really a mistake if you love it and it makes you feel fantastic. Remember: What looks best on you *is* what's best—it's not necessarily the most expensive item. Buy the garments you love, treat them with care, and they'll last a long time.

Pulling an Outfit Apart

Most people think about putting an outfit together. It sounds counterintuitive, but I advocate for pulling an outfit apart. That's because most of us get stuck in a rut, always wearing our outfits in unvarying ways: the same shirt and the same pair of pants with the same shoes. It worked once before and it looked good—so why upset the apple (or clothing) cart?

But pulling apart your outfits is the best thing you can do to expand your wardrobe—you'll find so many more outfit options that way. And now, because you're washing your entire wardrobe in one day, all your clothes will be available to you at once. You'll be able to look at everything together and reimagine your outfits in fresh, new ways.

Looking for inspiration? Here are some ideas:

First, the next time you shop in a favorite clothing store, go in with an open mind and ask for help from the employee who looks like she really loves clothes—the one who looks pulled to-gether but in a personal way. For example, ask for help from the guy who's wearing a great suit paired with Converse sneakers and a colorful tie rather than the sales rep dressed from head to toe in Armani (although I do love Armani—Armani is a genius). Then welcome his or her recommendations—even if you need to mull them over for a day or two. Who knows? You might dis-cover something that looks absolutely amazing on you that you'd never previously have given a second glance.

Second, take a good look at the people whose everyday style you admire. Make a mental note when you're at work or out for dinner, or surf online for images of outfits that you're drawn to. Then put together your own versions of these ensembles. If you're drawn to those styles, chances are you've got similar pieces in your closet already—maybe you've just never combined them in such a way. Now just put your own spin on them.

Third, consider buying inexpensive basics, like T-shirts and polos, from manufacturers whose quality you can count on. Then mix them in with your higher-quality, perhaps more-expensive, items. This high-low fashion approach is one I rely on often. For example, I have no problem wearing a discount-store polo under my Zang Toi cardigan.

I take this high-low approach with my clients' clothes as well. A few years ago, my friend and client Cassie—always eclectic and sophisticated in her fashion choices—had been invited to an evening party at a horse farm and didn't know what to wear. I cautioned her that the outfit I planned to pull for her was a little extra, even kind of risky. "Ship it," she said, and soon Cassie was slipping on a denim shirt and a wide western belt mixed with a white-lace beaded skirt that was pure eveningwear. I assumed she'd wear her turquoise jewelry, which she did, and her cowboy boots, which she didn't. She did one better—wearing brown alligator pumps that were far more luxe. Perfect.

Here's a high-low example from my college days: A friend of mine wore sweatshirts and jeans day in and day out, and he was looking to up his style game. So I helped him find a great navy suit—not that he'd likely wear the suit as such very often. Instead, I showed him how he could wear the pieces separately: the jacket with a T-shirt, sweater vest (à la Chandler from *Friends*), and jeans; or the navy trousers with a shirt and a sweater. It was a great starting point for building his wardrobe.

Maybe you're transitioning from academia to the corporate world. No matter your gender, a great suit or even two great suits that can be used interchangeably (e.g., the pastel jacket with the black pants or the black blazer with the pastel skirt) make a thoughtful investment.

Now, to sum up: When no clothing is off-limits (due to your ability to care for it), shopping is much more fun. Wear everything you own. Discover your own special garment (mine is the cardigan). Don't be afraid to pull an outfit apart. Shop with an open mind. Take note of people whose style you admire. And consider buying inexpensive basics for a high-low approach to your outfits.

I'll close this chapter with my store's "codes of the house." Great French fashion houses, such as Dior and Saint Laurent, establish rules that define them and the look of their brands. In the industry, these are referred to as codes of the house. Mona Williams's current codes follow:

- Orange is a neutral.
- Your girlfriends are perfect for advice about TV shows; your gay friends are perfect for advice about shoes.
- As you walk out of the house, take a look in the mirror and then add one more thing.
- Calories in candy don't count.
- Missoni matches everything.
- Pattern-on-pattern matching is easy; monochromatic is hard.
- Leggings aren't pants.

☺ Go big or go home. (This especially applies to diamonds and handbags.)

☺ If you want it and don't know where to wear it, it's perfect for the grocery store.

☺ A motorcycle jacket looks great over everything.

☺ Taste is for cowards.

☺ Carrots are the best vegetable. Period.

☺ We, like the French, love jolie laide as the perfect sort of fashion sense. We just use the American term "ugly pretty" (i.e., like Prada—weird but chic).

☺ Shopping should be more fun than a birthday party— even a party with a pony.

12

Love and Laundry Are Universal

First enlightenment, then the laundry.

—GAUTAMA BUDDHA

I often end Laundry Camp by sharing a final hack—one that harkens back to the idea of those bossy clothes, demanding that you dry clean or handwash or dry flat, etc. But this trick is also a shopping tip. And it works every time.

So here's what you do: When you're afraid of the care instructions of a garment you really want, buy it anyway. Then, when you're back at home, lay the item out on your kitchen counter and take a pair of scissors from your junk drawer. Now, ever so carefully, snip that tag right off. There—now that item can't boss you around. And you can care for it exactly the way you know how.

There's a bigger life lesson in here. So often, we do—or don't do—things based on fear, when, actually, if we just believed in ourselves, and in others, we would find a better way forward. A way that makes our lives easier and our outlooks sunnier. If we cut out the things that are negative or cause stress, our attitudes brighten.

Since starting this book, the idea of doing laundry as an act of love has only grown stronger in me. I remember when my wonderful granddad died. Our neighbor knew that our family was distraught over his loss and understood that the funeral was rapidly approaching. She came knocking on our door and offered to do our laundry—all the washing, drying, folding, and pressing—everything for all of us. We still talk about her generous gift of service.

You might be surprised to learn that my partner, Ross, does our laundry most of the time. He does it because he cares. He knows how important caring for our clothes is to me and he steps up in every way. I can't explain how much that means to me. I appreciate it every single time he does this loving thing.

Consider how many people around the world would welcome the chance to wear freshly laundered clothes—and just how much dignity that offers. Yet so often we take this privilege for granted. Or think about a natural disaster—being able to wash and dry clothes and then, most importantly, wear clean clothes are often the first steps toward returning life to normal. Offering laundering to individuals in need has been a mission of mine, and one that's moved me to support the donation of washers and dryers to organizations serving homeless individuals and families.

You can view laundry as a chore and slog through it, begrudgingly and resentfully. Or you can change your attitude, and do it with zest and spunk and love. A chore is not a chore if you have fun doing it or if it makes you happy.

I don't think I'm overstating it to say that laundry is a metaphor for life. In fact, so many aspects of laundry can teach us life lessons. Consider these six:

1. Don't let those care tags be the boss of you. You call the shots and you're in charge—of your laundry and your life.

2. When we sort, we consider each item individually, but our wardrobes aren't complete until they're back in our closets. In short, we must recognize that we're all in this together. It's only then that we are whole.

3. Removing a stain is no big deal. Translation? Don't give up when you've made a mistake. You can fix it and move forward.

4. Shop with no limits. In life, be courageous in going after what you want—even your wildest dreams.

5. Certain items require special care. They're precious—just like you and your loved ones. Sometimes our family members and friends need special loving care. And sometimes we need to be gentle with ourselves.

6. Caring about your clothes is caring about the environment. In other words, your decisions have much broader impacts—on you, your community, and the whole world.

It was *Star Tribune* reporter Aimee Blanchette who first dubbed me the Laundry Evangelist. I was hoping for the Suds

Stud (kidding), but the name stuck and I'm glad it did. I do evangelize about laundry, and I truly believe that everything improves when you can do your laundry and do it well. This is my calling.

Not long ago, I was a speaker at a home show. I was heading back to my hotel when a group of brawny guys stopped me. They wanted tips for doing their laundry and they asked lots of great questions. This happens all the time, and it no longer surprises me who is interested in laundry. Nearly everyone is, and nearly everyone cares about doing it well. No matter your age (I got started in toddlerhood), sex, gender, race, religion, nationality, or other characteristics, pretty much everyone at least thinks about laundry. Laundry is universal.

That brings me full circle. Who could have guessed that a grandmother and a grandson hanging laundry on a line in the mid-1970s could start this movement of laundry love? With her big heart, her fearlessness, and her environmental approach to everything, Granny Dude invited me to help her. She never cared if I dropped an item on the ground (even if it meant she'd have to wash it again) or if my helping made her morning of laundry last much longer than she'd anticipated. She loved me, loved spending time with me, and loved to show me how to do my laundry.

Here's my parting thought: You don't *have* to do laundry— you *get* to do laundry. And when you do laundry for others, it's all the sweeter. That may sound trite, but it's the gospel truth.

Appendix I

Laundry Love's Recipes (Worth Every Stain)

Maxine's Punch

1 package regular lemonade Kool-Aid
1 package cherry Kool-Aid
12 ounces frozen orange juice, thawed
½ cup sugar (Domino brand preferred)
64 ounces pineapple juice, unsweetened
2 liters 7UP

Mix all ingredients, except for the 7UP, and freeze in a round bowl. When ready, place the frozen punch into a punch bowl, add 7UP, and serve.

Wilma's Wedding Almond Punch

4 packages cherry Jell-O

3 cups sugar

4 cups hot water

6 packages strawberry Kool-Aid

1 small bottle almond extract

2 large cans pineapple juice

2 cans frozen lemonade (plus water to make the lemonade)

12 ounces 7UP

Vanilla ice cream (optional)

Dissolve Jell-O and sugar in hot water. Mix in all other ingredients except the 7UP, and freeze in a round bowl. When ready, place the frozen punch into a punch bowl, add 7UP, and serve. If you wish, mix vanilla ice cream into the punch or add a small serving of vanilla ice cream to each glass.

Granny Dude's Blue Cheese Spread

16 ounces cream cheese

6 ounces blue cheese crumbles

1 medium onion, finely chopped

2 boiled eggs, chopped

¼–½ cup mayonnaise (enough to make it spreadable)

Loaf of fresh rye bread

Mix all ingredients, except the bread, with a hand mixer or in a stand mixer until creamy. Refrigerate before serving. Serve on rye bread.

Patric's Country-Style Barbecued Ribs

1 pound of country-style ribs per person

2 tablespoons water

1 onion, chopped

Barbecue sauce of your choice

While this started as my mom's recipe (Wilma's), I'm claiming it, because I make these ribs so often. We use country-style ribs, because they're meatier than baby back ribs. Trust me— these are a million times better.

Place the ribs in a slow cooker with a tiny amount of water— just a couple of tablespoons—and a chopped onion. Cook on low for at least six hours and up to eight hours. Use a meat thermometer to make sure they're done (180°F or so).

Remove the ribs from the slow cooker and lay them on a platter. Then generously brush the ribs, front and back, with your favorite barbecue sauce. While I often make my own barbecue sauce, I've been just as happy with bottled sauce. Now, here's the magic: Place the ribs on your grill and cook for roughly eight minutes (no need to flip) until the barbecue sauce caramelizes onto the ribs.

Serve with mashed potatoes, peas, and fried apples. Dig in, and don't worry about the stains. Then nap.

Granny Jiles's Sweet Potato Balls

4 large sweet potatoes
½ stick butter
¼ teaspoon salt

Boil sweet potatoes in water with butter and salt until tender. Drain and mash. Set aside.

½ teaspoon cinnamon
¼ teaspoon nutmeg
½ cup packed brown sugar
¼ cup white sugar
½ stick butter softened
½ cup chopped pecans
1 cup crushed pineapple, drained until dry
1 box corn flakes, crushed

Mix all ingredients except for the corn flakes into the sweet potatoes with a wooden spoon until well blended. Form into eight balls. Then roll each ball in crushed corn flakes until well covered. Once again, set aside.

2 tablespoons butter for buttering dish
1 can of pineapple rings, well drained
1 bag of miniature marshmallows

Butter the baking dish and then place eight well-drained pineapple rings in a single layer in the dish. Place one sweet potato ball on each ring and then top each ball with three marshmallows.

Bake at 350°F for 20 minutes. Serves eight.

Arlene's Sour Cream Pound Cake with Wilma's Chocolate Sauce

1 cup butter, softened

3 cups sugar

6 large eggs

3 cups all-purpose flour

¼ teaspoon baking soda

8 ounces sour cream

1 teaspoon vanilla extract

1 teaspoon almond extract

Beat the butter with an electric mixer at medium speed for about 2 minutes or until creamy. Gradually add the sugar, beating for 5 to 7 minutes. Add eggs one at a time, beating just until the yellow disappears.

Combine the flour and baking soda; gradually add the flour mixture to the creamed butter, alternating with sour cream; begin and end with the flour mixture. Mix at low speed, until just blended after each addition. Stir in flavorings.

Pour batter into a greased and floured 10-inch tube pan. Bake at 325°F for 1 hour and 20 minutes or until a wooden toothpick inserted into the center comes out clean.

Cool in the pan on a wire rack for 15 minutes. Remove from

the pan and let cool completely on a wire rack. Serve with chocolate sauce.

> *Chocolate Sauce:*
>
> 2 ¼ cups granulated sugar (Domino brand preferred)
> ¾ cup unsweetened Hershey's cocoa powder
> 1 ½ tablespoons all-purpose flour
> ¼ teaspoon salt
> 1 ½ cups whole milk
> 1 teaspoon vanilla

Place sugar, cocoa, flour, and salt in a medium saucepan along with ½ cup milk. Whisk to combine into a thick paste. Add remaining milk, whisk to blend thoroughly, and bring mixture to a boil. Then reduce heat to low and simmer very gently for 5 minutes, whisking constantly. Remove from heat, add the vanilla, and let the sauce cool. To serve, drizzle the sauce over individual slices of pound cake.

Cover and store any leftover sauce in the refrigerator for up to two weeks; you may warm the sauce in the microwave or on the stovetop. You can also mix the sauce with milk for great hot chocolate.

Wilma's Legendary Pumpkin Roll

> *Cake:*
>
> 3 eggs
> 1 cup sugar

⅔ cup pumpkin

1 teaspoon baking soda

½ teaspoon cinnamon

¾ cup self-rising flour

1 cup nuts (your choice)

Mix together all of the cake ingredients except for the nuts. Then spread the mixture on greased wax paper and sprinkle with the nuts. Bake at 350°F for 15 minutes and then cool on a baking rack.

Filling:

2 tablespoons butter

8 ounces cream cheese

¾ teaspoon vanilla

1 cup plus 2 tablespoons powdered sugar

While the cake cools, mix together all of the filling ingredients, except for the 2 tablespoons of powdered sugar. Spread the filling onto the cake and roll it up. Sprinkle with the additional powdered sugar, and serve.

Roberta's Bourbon Balls

7 tablespoons butter

1 pound sugar

¼ cup bourbon

5 squares of Baker's semisweet chocolate

50 or so whole pecans

Cream the butter. Then work in the sugar, followed by the bourbon. Roll the mixture into one-inch balls and freeze.

While the balls freeze, melt the chocolate in a double boiler. Then, using a toothpick, dip each frozen ball in the chocolate and set on wax paper. When you remove the toothpick, place a whole pecan on the top to cover the hole. Makes about 48 balls.

Appendix II

SIX LAUNDRY MYTHS

Here's a rundown of half a dozen laundry myths that often blow the minds of Laundry Campers. A few were covered in previous pages, and a few are new. Perhaps you, too, will find yourself amazed.

Laundry myth: Bleach whitens dingy white towels. Nope! Chlorine bleach actually *makes* your whites dingy. White textiles are dyed white, and so bleach removes the white dye, returning them to their original cotton color. (See "The Big White Lie," page 34.)

Laundry myth: You should handwash tights and pantyhose. Just throw each into a mesh bag and machine-wash by color—white, black, cool, or warm. Then hang to dry. Now, wasn't that easy?

Laundry myth: Dress shirts must be ironed. Whether or not you iron dress shirts is up to you. Honestly, some people like a bit of a rumpled look—that's fine. Other folks rarely wear dress shirts but break out the iron for special occasions, such as a job interview or wedding. Still others like a crisply ironed shirt practically every day of the week. All that said, if you don't ever see yourself ironing, consider buying no-iron dress shirts. These days, killer options are available at all price points, and they look great right out of the dryer.

Laundry myth: You should revive stretched-out sweaters by washing, even if still clean. Happily, this isn't true. Simply hang up the sweater and lightly use a steamer to bring back its shape.

Laundry myth: Dishwashing liquid removes stains. Dishwashing liquid is formulated to remove greasy stains, like burned-on mac and cheese from a casserole dish. It's not designed to lift a stain from your favorite sweater, and its chemical makeup is too harsh for nearly all fabrics. In fact, it can ruin clothes: I remember a popular meteorologist calling me one morning to ask how to remove a stain from a dressy jumpsuit she'd worn to a party the night before. Unfortunately, by then she'd already taken the advice of a friend who'd advised using dishwashing liquid. It was too late—the dish soap had removed both the stain *and* the dye from the treatment area, and ruined the garment.

Laundry myth: Your dryer eats socks. Of course this isn't true. The dryer is a picky eater—it only gobbles up one from your favorite pair.

Appendix III

LAUNDRY ICONS

Now you know practically everything there is to know about cleaning your textiles. But in case you're interested in the meanings of all those little international icons on your garment care tags, here's a guide to help you understand. Just remember: Don't let your clothes tell you what to do!

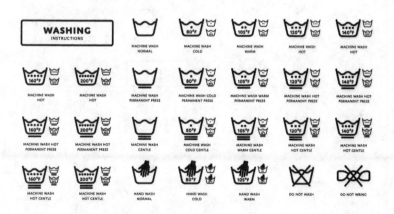

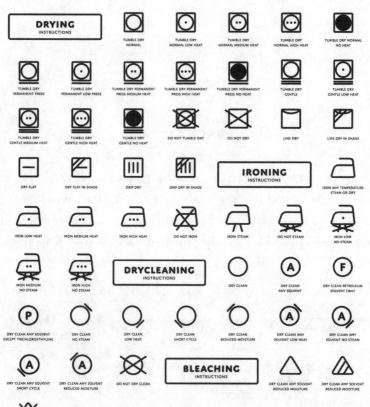

DRYING INSTRUCTIONS

TUMBLE DRY NORMAL

TUMBLE DRY NORMAL LOW HEAT

TUMBLE DRY NORMAL MEDIUM HEAT

TUMBLE DRY NORMAL HIGH HEAT

TUMBLE DRY NORMAL NO HEAT

TUMBLE DRY PERMANENT PRESS

TUMBLE DRY PERMANENT LOW PRESS

TUMBLE DRY PERMANENT PRESS MEDIUM HEAT

TUMBLE DRY PERMANENT PRESS HIGH HEAT

TUMBLE DRY PERMANENT PRESS NO HEAT

TUMBLE DRY GENTLE

TUMBLE DRY GENTLE LOW HEAT

TUMBLE DRY GENTLE MEDIUM HEAT

TUMBLE DRY GENTLE HIGH HEAT

TUMBLE DRY GENTLE NO HEAT

DO NOT TUMBLE DRY

DO NOT DRY

LINE DRY

LINE DRY IN SHADE

DRY FLAT

DRY FLAT IN SHADE

DRIP DRY

DRIP DRY IN SHADE

IRONING INSTRUCTIONS

IRON ANY TEMPERATURE STEAM OR DRY

IRON LOW HEAT

IRON MEDIUM HEAT

IRON HIGH HEAT

DO NOT IRON

IRON STEAM

DO NOT STEAM

IRON LOW NO STEAM

IRON MEDIUM NO STEAM

IRON HIGH NO STEAM

DRYCLEANING INSTRUCTIONS

DRY CLEAN

DRY CLEAN ANY SOLVENT

DRY CLEAN PETROLEUM SOLVENT ONLY

DRY CLEAN ANY SOLVENT EXCEPT TRICHLOROETHYLENE

DRY CLEAN NO STEAM

DRY CLEAN LOW HEAT

DRY CLEAN SHORT CYCLE

DRY CLEAN REDUCED MOISTURE

DRY CLEAN ANY SOLVENT LOW HEAT

DRY CLEAN ANY SOLVENT NO STEAM

DRY CLEAN ANY SOLVENT SHORT CYCLE

DRY CLEAN ANY SOLVENT REDUCED MOISTURE

DO NOT DRY CLEAN

BLEACHING INSTRUCTIONS

DRY CLEAN ANY SOLVENT REDUCED MOISTURE

DRY CLEAN ANY SOLVENT REDUCED MOISTURE

DRY CLEAN ANY SOLVENT REDUCED MOISTURE

Acknowledgments

All of us have special ones who loved us into being.
—FRED ROGERS,
TV PERSONALITY, WRITER,
PRODUCER, MINISTER

Patric and Karin wish to express our deepest appreciation to everyone at Flatiron Books, particularly Bob Miller and Amy Einhorn (now at Henry Holt), whose excitement for this project let us know we were onto something; Sarah Murphy, whose thoughtful questions and detailed editing made this a better, stronger read; Claire McLaughlin and Amelia Possanza for all of their publicity efforts; plus the entire editorial, marketing, publicity, and production teams—we're so grateful for everything you've done to make *Laundry Love* a success. Thanks, too, to Katy Robitzski of Macmillan Audio, who shepherded our audiobook. A heartfelt thank-you goes out to all the pros at the Levine Greenberg Rostan Literary Agency—especially Daniel Greenberg, who immediately believed in our vision for the book, and Tim Wojcik, who led the effort to get *Laundry Love* into hands around the world. We're thankful for Zach Harris, whose charming and lighthearted illustrations so fittingly reflect our content. And we'd be remiss if we didn't declare our indebtedness to Chuck Klosterman, who trusted us enough to connect us with his (and now our) literary agent. Finally, thanks to the Caribou Coffee team at Mall of America (South Skyway)—we appreciate every hour we got to make your meeting room our satellite office (thanks for the coffee and treats, too).

Patric wishes to thank:
First, I have to again mention Ross. He made this book possible by supporting me throughout the entire process. He believed in me and my store from the very beginning; without his belief, I wouldn't have had this opportunity.

Second, Karin Miller . . . what can I say? Without you, this book may never have been—so many hours at Caribou Coffee and so many phone calls! Working with you has been a true honor, and totally my pleasure.

The people who make (or have made) my store run: Marsha Sussman, Hadass Sveback, Jessica Hastie, Kelsey Campion, Erik Rice, Emily Dufault, Siah Camara, Rachel Solares, Ellie Burdorf, Gina Romans, Daina Amborn, Tresa Garr, Luna Fredericks, Aurora Anderson, and Martha Gingras. Without all of you supporting the store and me, we wouldn't be here. Thank you all so much for showing the customers how great laundry and laundry products can be. And thanks, too, to all of my Laundry Campers for their insightful questions, great enthusiasm, and good humor.

People who've been kind enough to cover me in the media: Aimee Blanchette (thanks for the title and for the start in the laundry world), Nancy Ngo, Kathy Berdan, Allison Kaplan,

Heidi Raschke, Jahna Peloquin, Lori Barghini, Julie Cobbs, Karen Schneider, Chris Hrapsky, Julie Nelson, Lesley Kennedy, Joel Seidman, Kevin Tibbles, Chris Dukas, Brittany Larson, Lisa Adams, Steve Patterson, Elizabeth Ries, Heather Brown, Frank Vascellaro, Amelia Santaniello, Nicole Aksamit Purcell, Ashley Abramson, Sue Campbell, Donna Bulseco, and Kyle Erickson (your article helped launch the book!).

People who pushed my career forward: Amy Bishop, Meghan Haapala, Mary Riley Caufield, John Banks, Saeteesh, Melissa Herrig, Diana Storey, Carla Holzer, Katie Young, Shannon Duckworth, Courtney Ursetti, and Heather Ryan; Daune Stinson, Jennifer Carnahan, Connor Koerbitz, Therese Thull, and Suzanne Garry; Ron Boaz and Tom Bruenderman; Zang Toi, Mark Mallman, and Christine Jones; Melissa Smith, Katie Williams, Katie Turcotte, Arleigh Hagberg, Amy Sperling, MaryAnn Goldstein, Leisl Auvante, Lauren Lieber, Lantz and Kiley Powell, Gayle Erickson, Rebecca Bell Sorenson, and Kathy Ekberg; Lisa Taylor and the Ghermazian Brothers at Mall of America (thanks for the chance!); Chris Navrati and Shamrock Productions (thank you for believing in Laundry Camp early on).

Three people I wish could've read the book: Roxann Nelson, Jim Schaal, and Taylor Lieber (your memories were with me through it).

Finally, Diane Ferguson, Cassie Harpel, Mark Bradford, Raleigh Glassberg, Seth McNaughton, Sarah Prutzman, Heather Sauber, Ellen Shafer, Glenna Maggard; John, Erin, and Matthew Rodriguez; Tim, Laura, Lee, and Walker Riddle; Marc Raihala, Todd, and Carmel Lehnard; of course, Ben and Reagan, Suzanne Hall, Jarrod Richardson, Harmie Justice, and Nancy Richardson; and last, but with utmost importance, my parents, Ron

Richardson and Wilma Justice, who thought it was a good idea to give a three-year-old a washing machine!

Karin wishes to thank:

Patric—your kindness, creativity, and wit, plus your easygoing approach to my copy made writing this book a complete joy. (I look forward to getting that pool key.)

Thom, who lives his values, adores our children, and champions my every project; and Gabi, Joey, and Mia, for whom I'm thankful every day, who constantly amaze me with your interests and accomplishments, and whom I've been lucky enough to watch grow up. Thanks to each of you for listening during so many read-aloud sessions. I love each of you so much!

My mom, a children's book author and elementary school teacher, who inspired my own writing and whose tendency to shrink my wool sweaters sparked me into doing my own laundry back in high school; and my dad, the very best of men who still encourages the dreams of his children and grandchildren every single day. Even as adults, whenever my sister, my brother, or I needed them, they'd still jump in, helping in whatever way they could. For my mom, that often entailed doing countless loads of laundry for my family, especially when Thom was fighting cancer while I was pregnant, and after the birth of each of our three kids. All my love to you!

Gaye, Andrew, Tony, Jim, Denise, Anna, Nate, and Risa— so appreciate and love each one of you; Jane, Mark, Mary, and David—thanks for your love and support (right back at you!); all of the Norlins, especially Aunt Sandra, who has always believed in my writing; Murray Brandys, who first invited me to tell his story in a memoir; Sara Chastain, who accompanied me to my first Laundry Camp (two years before I approached Patric about writing this book!); Bryn Larson, who generously helped with the book proposal; The Lacek Group, especially Shawn, Karen, Lizzie, Wendy, and Carolyn, who always make work so much fun; my favorite clients, the City of Eagan and University of Minnesota teams (especially Tom Garrison, Joe Ellickson, Joanna Foote, Emily Katsuma, Ashley Lawson, and Elizabeth Patty), who understood when I needed to take a few months off to finish the book; Augie girls for your lifelong support and friendships; and my SLP friends, especially the Yosemiteam (young and not so young).